NEW GUINEA

The Allied Jungle Campaign in World War II

Jon Diamond

STACKPOLE
BOOKS

Published by
STACKPOLE BOOKS
5067 Ritter Road
Mechanicsburg, PA 17055
www.stackpolebooks.com

Printed in the United States of America

10 9 8 7 6 5 4 3 2 1

Cover design by Caroline Stover

Library of Congress Cataloging-in-Publication Data

Diamond, Jon (Jonathan Russell)
  New Guinea : the Allied jungle campaign in World War II / Jon Diamond.
      pages cm — (Stackpole military photo series)
  ISBN 978-0-8117-1556-0
1. World War, 1939–1945—Campaigns—New Guinea. 2. World War, 1939–1945—Jungle warfare. I. Title.
  D767.95.D53 2015
  940.54'265—dc23
                                          2014049996

CONTENTS

On next page: After nearly a decade of military action in China, the Japanese Empire embarked on its bold mission to establish hegemony over the countries and island chains shown here, which were mostly under the control or influence of Britain, the United States, Australia, and the Netherlands government-in-exile. This map depicts the massive extent of Japan's conquest and ultimate ambitions at the high-water mark through the summer of 1942. With the exceptions of battles at the Coral Sea, Midway, and Milne Bay, the overland Port Moresby assault, and the failure to quickly defeat an isolated American 1st Marine Division on Guadalcanal, almost all of Imperial Japan's initial strategic goals were achieved. PHILIP SCHWARTZBERG, MERIDIAN MAPPING

CHAPTER 1
STRATEGIC OVERVIEW

After the carrier attack by the Imperial Japanese Navy (IJN) on Pearl Harbor, Hawaii, on December 7, 1941, the Imperial Japanese Army (IJA) conducted offensive operations across a broad front of 7,000 miles, from Singapore to Midway Island. The success of Adm. Chuichi Nagumo's aerial assault on the anchorage of the United States Pacific Fleet that fateful morning assured the Japanese complete naval supremacy in the Pacific Ocean. Early war-planning sessions set Malaya and Singapore as targets for the IJA's major thrust, while additional supporting operations were mounted to seize the Philippines, Guam, Hong Kong, and parts of British Borneo in the Western Pacific. Guam was occupied easily by December 8, 1941, and Wake Island fell on December 23 after a spirited fight from its Marine Defense Battalion.

The Japanese High Command had planned that once Malaya and Singapore were captured, these British bastions would serve as springboards to seize southern Sumatra and invade the Netherlands East Indies (NEI), where there were vast resources to supply Japan and its war effort. This had been occurring on the Asian mainland for almost a decade. Adding to the Japanese hegemony in the Pacific was the sinking of HMS *Prince of Wales* and HMS *Repulse* in the South China Sea. Dispatched by British prime minister Winston Churchill to serve as a deterrent to Japanese expansion, the pair were hit on December 10, 1941, by land-based Mitsubishi G4M Betty and Mitsubishi G3M Nell medium horizontal and torpedo-bearing bombers. Malaya and Singapore fell to a numerically inferior Japanese Twenty-Fifth Army, commanded by Lt. Gen. Tomoyuki Yamashita, on February 15, 1942, after only seventy days of resistance to the Japanese juggernaut down the Malay Peninsula and across the Strait of Johore to Singapore Island.

Australia had sent two brigades of its 8th Division to Malaya. After considerable fighting toward the end of

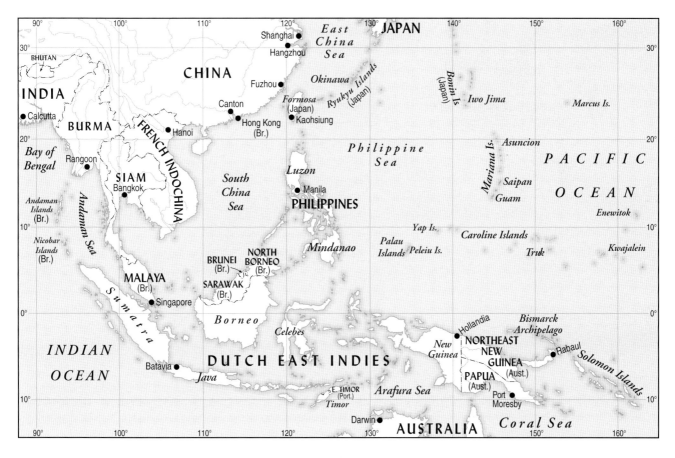

1

the campaign, the 15,000-man contingent was forced to surrender in mid-February with the rest of Singapore's garrison. The three remaining battalions of the Australian Imperial Force's (AIF) 8th Division were sent to reinforce the Dutch at Amboina, Timor, and Rabaul; however, these units were overrun by the Japanese.

Even before the collapse of Malaya, the first Japanese air attack against Rabaul, in northern New Britain, occurred on January 21, 1942, with over 100 Japanese fighters and bombers attacking the main Australian air base in the Bismarck Archipelago, northeast of New Guinea. Eight out of ten RAAF Wirraway fighters (essentially American AT-6 Texan trainers) and three Lockheed Hudson bombers were annihilated. On the night of January 22–23, Maj. Gen. Tomitaro Horii's 5,300-strong South Seas Detachment steamed into Rabaul Harbor on the northern tip of New Britain. The Australian defenders put up a brave fight but eventually withdrew. As the Japanese overran northern New Britain in the ensuing days, most of the Aus-

tralians were brutally massacred or died as prisoners. The RAAF chief at Rabaul evacuated the remainder of his air detachment—two surviving Wirraways and one Lockheed Hudson bomber—back to Australia. Now all that was left separating Australia from the Japanese offensive were a few Australian troops in the Bulolo Valley and the garrison at Port Moresby on the southern coast of Papua New Guinea. Rabaul would become the headquarters for the Japanese Eighth Area Army, with five airfields and a harbor that could serve as anchorage for a large part of the IJN.

Across the Arafura Sea from Papua lay the arid Northern Territories of the Australian continent. Since it was prevailing American military wisdom that the Philippines could not be held if the Japanese mounted a full-scale attack on them, extensive preparations were not made prior to Gen. Douglas MacArthur's arrival in 1935 to command the Philippine forces. Over the next six years, the buildup of forces under his leadership was quite tardy, and U.S. and Philippine army strength

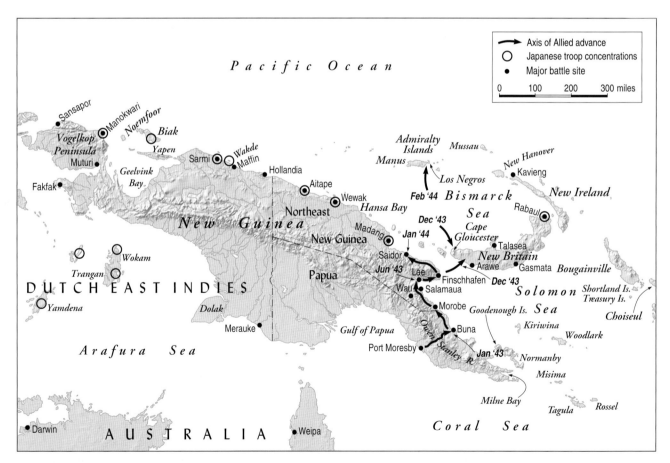

New Guinea, the world's second largest island, is divided into three main parts: Papua to the southeast, Northeast New Guinea, and Netherlands New Guinea to the west. This map also shows the surrounding islands of the Dutch East Indies, the northern Solomon Islands, the Bismarck Archipelago, New Ireland, and the Admiralty Islands. The northern coast of New Guinea, including adjacent islands and the Vogelkop Peninsula, would comprise the remainder of General MacArthur's 1944 campaign to capture and build airfields after "leapfrogging" over Japanese strongholds in his drive to get into position for finally launching his return to the Philippine Islands. PHILIP SCHWARTZBERG, MERIDIAN MAPPING

was far below what was necessary when the Japanese struck the archipelago. MacArthur's air strength was destroyed mostly on the ground at Clark Field near Manila by Japanese bombers based in Formosa within hours of the attack on Pearl Harbor, and its remnants quickly succumbed to attrition by a superior aerial foe. Although the Japanese expected a quick victory in the Philippines, largely due to their air and naval dominance, MacArthur's American and Filipino troops retreated into the Bataan Peninsula and held out there until April 9, 1942. The neighboring island fortress of Corregidor in Manila Bay finally capitulated on May 6 after a Japanese invasion.

In early January 1942, Field Marshal Sir Archibald Wavell was appointed Supreme Commander of ABDACOM—the cumbersome new combined American, British, Dutch, and Australian command, to be headquartered on Java—after Churchill designated him Commander in Chief (CIC) Far East on December 30, 1941. This command was ludicrous since it encompassed all Allied forces in Burma, Singapore, Malaya, the Dutch East Indies, the Philippines (which Wavell never assumed control of), and North West Australia. However, American Army Chief of Staff Gen. George Marshall's operational goal was to have a single supreme commander in each war theater. In order to persuade a reluctant Churchill of his command structure concept, Marshall offered that Wavell should be the supreme commander for the whole of the Far East theater, i.e. ABDA. Churchill sent Wavell a long, coded telegram outlining the job: "The President and his military and naval advisers have impressed on me the urgent need for a unified command in South West Pacific." Fortunately, the onerous ABDA command was disbanded on February 22, 1942, since by that time Hong Kong, Singapore, Malaya, the Dutch East Indies, and other possessions were already lost.

Before the fall of Singapore, Japanese units had started their conquest of the NEI, despite the fact that the local Dutch government had over 100,000 men available. Unfortunately, this large force was spread out piecemeal across the major islands of the Indonesian archipelago. The ABDA air force and naval detachments, the latter under Adm. Thomas Hart, were quickly dispatched in the Battle of the Java Sea. Tarakan Island fell on January 10, 1942, followed by the capture of Borneo and Sumatra. Java ended its resistance on March 8. After the loss of the NEI, American general George Brett, who had been Wavell's chief American deputy in the ABDA command, was appointed the commander of all U.S. forces in Australia. At this point, most of the force was comprised of air units that had landed in Australia after fleeing the Philippines and NEI.

Finally, southern Burma was invaded in April 1942 with the intent of defeating the British and Indian forces there in order to sever the Burma Road and thus Chiang Kai-shek and his army's supply lifeline through the Burmese port of Rangoon.

Ironically, the IJA used only eleven of its fifty-one divisions during these offensive operations in southern Asia, reserving the majority for home defense, the protracted offensives on the Chinese mainland, and as a sufficient force in Manchuria to counter any possible Soviet moves against Japan there. Still, Imperial Japan's high-water mark had not yet been reached.

The Japanese were now presented with a military decision borne of their string of rapid conquests: namely, should there be further expansion southward to cut the long supply lines from the United States to Australia and New Zealand, in effect isolating the Antipodes. The IJA decided to move southward from NEI in mid-January, first to New Britain with the seizure of Rabaul, and from there the occupation of key positions in Papua New Guinea. By doing so, the Japanese High Command left the South Pacific supply routes open to Australia, an omission they would later need to remedy by seizing the Solomon Island chain.

Darwin, an administrative seat in the Northern Territories of Australia, was now under direct threat of the advancing Japanese. It was also a terminus for European airlines to Australia and a major seaport in the north. Most of the Australian army was in the Middle East, serving first in the Western Desert Force and later as the Eighth Army under Auchinleck and Montgomery; the Australian government could only spare modest reinforcements for Darwin's garrison of 14,000 men and the couple of RAAF squadrons stationed there. At the time of the Pearl Harbor attack, 121,000 men of the AIF were serving overseas, leaving only 37,000 to defend Australia. The RAAF had suffered grievously in Malaya and Singapore, losing 165 planes and leaving only 175 for Australia's defense. Aside from Catalina patrol bombers and 53 Lockheed Hudson bombers, the majority of RAAF planes were Wirraways. Darwin was bombed by the Japanese for the first time on February 19, 1942, four days after British lieutenant general Arthur Percival surrendered Singapore with a sizeable contingent of the AIF, which had figured largely in the prewar defense planning for Australia.

Australian prime minister John Curtin wanted his AIF divisions in the Middle East to return home for the defense of Australia. Two brigades of the AIF 6th Division were temporarily transferred to Ceylon while the

Papua, the Huon Peninsula of Northeast New Guinea, and the southwestern portion of New Britain in the Bismarck Archipelago. The dashed line denotes the Allied advance along the Kokoda Trail, which started in late September 1942, and the subsequent brutal assault on the Japanese positions at Buna, Gona, and Sanananda Point, which were not captured until early 1943. After the north coast of Papua was secured, Australian forces primarily contested the Japanese in Northeast New Guinea and the Huon Peninsula with some U.S. Army contingents and a paratroop assault at Nadzab. The refitted U.S. 1st Marine Division and U.S. Army troops assaulted Cape Gloucester and Arawe on southwest New Britain in December 1943. PHILIP SCHWARTZBERG, MERIDIAN MAPPING

division's remaining brigade and the AIF 7th Division returned to Australia; its leading elements arrived in mid-March 1942. With the AIF 9th Division remaining in the Middle East, Curtin was mollified by the green American 32nd and 41st Infantry Divisions being hastily deployed to Australia's defense. The 41st Division arrived in Australia in April 1942 and the 32nd in May.

The Japanese, with their major troop commitment to China and Manchuria, had for the time being abandoned any idea of invading Australia directly and instead planned to isolate the Northern Territories, along with Darwin and its harbor, by occupying Port Moresby on the southern coast of Papua. In early March 1942, Port Moresby had only the 30th Infantry Brigade, a field artillery regiment, and coastal and anti-aircraft artillery units, totaling between 6,000–7,000 men. On February 21, President Franklin D. Roosevelt cabled MacArthur on Corregidor and ordered him to leave for Mindanao and then proceed to Australia. On March 11, MacArthur and his retinue left Corregidor in four patrol torpedo (PT) boats and arrived at Mindanao. From there a fleet of B-17s in rough shape transported MacArthur's group to Batchelor Field, south of Darwin, on March 17.

Initially, rather than taking Port Moresby by an overland route, the IJN was to capture it in an amphibious operation, which was mitigated by a U.S. carrier task force at the Battle of the Coral Sea on May 4–8, 1942. Despite causing the loss of the USS *Lexington* and damaging the USS *Yorktown*, the Japanese invasion force retreated after one carrier was lost and another damaged. Many experienced IJN pilots died in the sea battle, the first fought solely by carrier-based planes.

After seizing Rabaul, the Japanese High Command was also interested in the Huon Gulf area on the north coast of Northeast New Guinea and Papua, the island's east end. Japanese staging moves to take Papua New Guinea began on March 8–11, 1942, when IJA and IJN elements landed at Salamaua, Lae, and Finschhafen on the Huon Gulf in Northeast New Guinea. Between April 1 and 20, Special Naval Landing Force (SNLF) troops landed in Fafak, Babo, Sorong, Manokwari, Momi, Nabire, Seroi, Sarmi, and Hollandia along the north coast of New Guinea.

On December 7, 1941, the Imperial Japanese Navy attacked Pearl Harbor on Oahu with six carriers under the command of Adm. Chuichi Nagumo. All of the U.S. Pacific Fleet's battleships were hit by torpedo or horizontal bombers. Military installations on shore such as airfields and army barracks also suffered grievously. Well over 2,000 sailors, soldiers, and airmen died as a result of the raid. Above, tugboats and salvage crews in ships' launches and whaleboats try to put out the raging fires aboard some of the stricken vessels as a search for survivors in the water is conducted. LIBRARY OF CONGRESS

Besides the battleships, a host of dry-docked naval vessels berthed in the Pearl Harbor Navy Yard were also struck by Japanese bombs or torpedoes that Sunday morning. Here, the destroyer USS *Shaw* is a raging inferno after several dive bombers of the second aerial assault wave attacked. The photograph shows the moment when the forward magazine exploded; the crew was ordered to abandon ship before the destroyer sank.
LIBRARY OF CONGRESS

American prisoners, some with their hands tied behind their back, are allowed a brief break during the Bataan Death March in April 1942. After a full-scale invasion of Luzon by the Japanese within days of the Pearl Harbor attack, American and Filipino soldiers were forced to retreat into a slim defensive position on the island's western Bataan Peninsula in January 1942. On April 9, the American and Filipino forces formally surrendered to the Japanese. Immediately after, the Japanese marched the 12,000 American and 64,000 Filipino prisoners northward on a 60-mile journey into captivity, committing atrocities along the route. The ordeal lasted from five to twelve days, with over 5,000 Americans dying along the way. LIBRARY OF CONGRESS

Fellow American and Filipino prisoners rigged litters to carry some of the wounded and sick to the prison camp. More often, however, the wounded and sick who could not continue the march were either executed by their Japanese captors or left at the side of the road to die, regardless of their nationality. NARA

A Japanese Special Naval Landing
Force (SNLF) reconnaissance party
observes Japanese artillery
bombardment of American and
Filipino positions after General
MacArthur's troops withdrew into
the Bataan Peninsula, where they
would mount a tenacious defense.
USAMHI

The Japanese invading force
captured thousands of American
and Filipino soldiers on Corregidor.
Here, survivors of the intense
Japanese bombardment and
invasion of the island are ushered
from the Malinta Tunnel, an
underground warren of infirmaries,
offices, machine shops, and
headquarters. The defenders in the
tunnel were able to withstand the
bombardment but not the assault of
the Japanese ground forces. NARA

Australia's extensive military commitments overseas in defense of the British Empire against the Axis Powers rendered the forces depleted at home to resist any Japanese aggressive move. Prime Minister Curtin was all too aware that he would need the assistance of the United States, especially after Britain's surrender at Singapore in mid-February 1942. Here, newly arrived Australian soldiers man a trench wearing every article of clothing they had on a cold night in the North African desert outside Bardia, waiting for their assault on the Italian town to begin during General Wavell's Operation COMPASS in December 1940. These men were from the Australian 6th Division, under the command of Maj. Gen. Iven Mackay, with its 16th, 17th, and 18th Brigades raised in New South Wales, Victoria, and Queensland, respectively. NARA

After the main defenses were penetrated at Bardia, Italian resistance crumbled. Here, a heavily garbed Australian 6th Division soldier takes the surrender from three Italians. He is carrying his Short Magazine Lee Enfield .303-inch rifle with attached sword bayonet. NARA

Australian soldiers are not only acclimatizing themselves to Western Desert conditions in this photograph but also learning basic armor/infantry tactics with light tanks of the Royal Tank Regiment. After adjusting to the desert climate, the Australians headed for the frontlines of Operation COMPASS outside of Bardia in mid-December, replacing the Indian 4th Division that was being sent to Eritrea under Gen. William Platt. NARA

An *ad hoc* Australian artillery crew mans a captured Italian fieldpiece and puts it to use firing on Rommel's advancing *Deutsche Afrika Korps* (DAK) during the siege of Tobruk, which began on April 11, 1941. The Australian 9th Division, under the command of Maj. Gen. Leslie Morshead, held the fortress of Tobruk ever since Rommel's forces had surrounded the port area. NARA

Australian 22nd Brigade troops of the AIF's 8th Division arrive in Singapore in February 1941 as the first contingent of Australia's ground troops to garrison the island. The 8th Division, under the command of Maj. Gen. Gordon Bennett, was one of four all-volunteer divisions. The other three—the 6th, 7th, and 9th—were fighting in the Middle East and would become a bone of contention between Prime Minister Curtin of Australia and British prime minister Winston Churchill when hostilities started at the end of the year. At the time of the Pearl Harbor attack, 121,000 men of the AIF were serving overseas, leaving only 37,000 to defend Australia. NARA

Field Marshal Sir Archibald Wavell (front row, second from left) salutes with other Allied commanders in Batavia (now Jakarta) on the island of Java upon his arrival there to assume the ABDA command, created on January 3, 1942. Wavell's new assignment was onerous given the geographical extent of the area he was to command. This was further complicated by the many nations and commanders that would be subordinate to him, as exemplified by MacArthur's retaining complete control of the American and Filipino forces in the Philippine Islands. USAMHI

ABDA Commander Field Marshal Wavell (right), with Gen. George Brett (left), American Forces commander in Australia, and Adm. Thomas Hart (center), commander of the U.S. Asiatic Fleet, on Java in mid-January 1942. Hart's fleet had fled from Cavite Naval Yard after a Japanese bombardment soon after Pearl Harbor. In order to promote Allied unity and organization structure, American Army Chief of Staff Gen. George C. Marshall and Churchill agreed to appoint Field Marshal Wavell as the supreme commander of the ill-fated ABDA command from early January to late February 1942. USAMHI

Australian antitank (AT) gunners manning a 2-pounder AT gun allow a column of Japanese tanks to get as close as possible before firing on them on the Muar-Bakri Road in Johore Province, Malaya, in January 1942. This was a preset ambush, and this particular crew accounted for five destroyed Japanese tanks. The Australian infantry showed no mercy to the surviving Japanese tank crewmembers who escaped from their disabled armored vehicles. NARA

Australian troops of the AIF 8th Division trek through the Malayan jungle in Johore Province. They had been at Endau and Mersing on Malaya's east coast in Johore, where they had built extensive defense positions and sown hundreds of mines. However, the Japanese bypassed Mersing, much to the chagrin of the Australian defenders. In addition to elements of this division serving under Percival in Malaya, the AIF's 8th Division's 3rd Brigade was deployed to Rabaul at the northern end of the island of New Britain and to Dutch East Indies' locales. All of these were soon to be conquered by Japanese troops. AWM

Brewster Buffalo fighters of RAAF 454 Squadron lined up wingtip to wingtip for a prewar photograph at an airstrip in Malaya. Although the pilot had armor protection, this fighter, the U.S. Navy's first monoplane fighter in 1938, was outclassed by both the IJA's Nate and Oscar fighters and the IJN's Zero. Nonetheless, the Australian pilots serving in Malaya and on Singapore flew heroically against the odds. It was erroneously believed that any Japanese amphibious assault on the Malay Peninsula could be stopped by Allied airpower as long as the infantry was able to protect the airfields from ground assault. What was neglected was an adequate antiaircraft defense network once the Japanese bombed and then seized the Allied airfields on Malaya's northeast coast for their own use. The Australian pilots and their planes were subsequently decimated in Malaya and Singapore, rendering North West Australia, particularly the port of Darwin, virtually defenseless against Japanese air raids. USAMHI

Dutch Air Force pilots from the Netherlands East Indies, flying an RAAF Lockheed Hudson, go over a flight plan for a reconnaissance mission to search for a Japanese invasion fleet before hostilities commenced. The Hudson was manufactured in the United States and given to Britain and Australia as part of Lend-Lease. It was developed as a six-seat coastal reconnaissance bomber with a limited bomb capacity of 1,350–1,600 pounds. For defense, it was armed with seven .303-inch machine guns scattered across the plane. Their presence, and subsequent destruction, in Malaya and Singapore would certainly limit Australia's ability to reconnoiter the northwest and eastern coasts should the fear of a Japanese amphibious assault ever materialize. NARA

In the late autumn of 1941, Churchill dispatched the Royal Navy's Force Z, comprised of the HMS *Prince of Wales*, the HMS *Repulse*, and a four-vessel flotilla of older British and Australian destroyers to Singapore to serve as a deterrent to Japanese expansion in the Far East and to placate Australia. Above is an aerial view from an attacking Japanese plane of the HMS *Prince of Wales* (top) and the battle cruiser HMS *Repulse* early in the attack on December 10, 1941. *Repulse* has just sustained a bomb hit, evidenced by the plume of black smoke rising from the ship. Several near misses are also apparent on both sides of the vessel. Within minutes torpedoes sank the *Repulse*; the *Prince of Wales* soon followed. NARA

The crew of HMS *Prince of Wales* abandoning their heavily listing battleship. Sailors hauled themselves onto the deck of HMS *Express*, from which this photograph was taken. Shortly after the photograph was taken, the lifelines had to be severed so that the sinking battleship would not capsize the much smaller destroyer. The myth of the battleship's invincibility to aerial assault and sinking was now finally ended. Other than a few U.S. destroyers and the cruiser USS *Houston*, there was no major Allied naval force in the western Pacific. Australia's fears about imminent Japanese movements toward their homeland suddenly increased exponentially. NARA

An Australian soldier is captured by the Japanese in Johore Province on the Malay Peninsula. He is being led away by a Japanese officer (left), identified by his pistol, map case, and traditional officer's sword carried in his right hand. After considerable fighting toward the end of the campaign in Johore Province, the 15,000-man contingent of the AIF's 8th Division was forced to surrender in mid-February with the rest of Singapore Island's garrison of British, Indian, Malay, and Singapore volunteer forces. AWM

The Australian 22nd and 27th Brigades of the AIF 8th Division bore the brunt of repelling the Japanese invasion force hurled across the Strait of Johore in the northwest corner of Singapore Island on February 8, 1942. Despite outnumbering the invader and still possessing sufficient ammunition, British lieutenant general Arthur Percival feared a civil calamity when his forces lost control of the island's water reservoirs and sought terms of surrender from his adversaries just one week later. Here, Japanese troops are photographed with their Australian and British prisoners, who would soon enter an extremely harsh and cruel captivity. USAMHI

At the Ford factory at Bukit Timah on Singapore Island on February 15, 1942, Lieutenant General Percival (middle of foreground row with back to camera) "negotiates" the terms of surrender with the victorious Japanese lieutenant general Tomoyuki Yamashita, who sits across from him (cap by his right hand). Yamashita would brook no delay in the negotiation, since he feared that his bluff with fewer troops and no artillery ammunition left would be discovered, thereby emboldening his British foe to continue fighting. Yamashita's staff knew that if the British and their Commonwealth forces kept up their defense of Singapore City and its outskirts, the Japanese would have to retreat to Johore Province to replenish their supplies, which would disrupt the strict timetable for the island's capture. USAMHI

Victorious Japanese troops, uncharacteristically in informal uniform, cheerily parade down a street in front of the General Post Office in newly occupied Singapore after the British surrender of the island on February 15, 1942. The length of the entire Japanese campaign, which commenced on December 8, 1941, was almost exactly 70 days—far more rapid than the Japanese Imperial General Staff's plan of 100 days. USAMHI

An aerial view of the Japanese invasion fleet, heading for Port Moresby in Papua New Guinea, taking evasive action from American carrier aircraft attacking them in the Battle of the Coral Sea on May 7, 1942. The Japanese had sunk the mighty USS *Lexington*, the oiler *Neosho*, and the destroyer USS *Sims*. In addition, another carrier, the USS *Yorktown*, was damaged and had to head to Pearl Harbor for repairs. The Americans had sunk only the carrier *Shoho* and damaged another Japanese carrier, *Shokaku*. This battle was a tactical victory for the Japanese but a strategic one for the U.S. Navy in that the Japanese invasion and occupation of Port Moresby, just north of Australia, was successfully prevented. One of the other salutary outcomes of the naval battle for the Americans was that the Japanese carrier *Zuikaku* was placed "in mothballs" upon returning to Japan, not because it was damaged, but because it had lost so many trained pilots that the carrier was not considered a good fighting vessel any longer.
NARA

The Japanese aircraft at the Battle of Coral Sea began attacking the USS *Lexington* at 1118 hours on May 7, 1942. Two minutes after the attack began, a torpedo struck the forward side and another hit just opposite the bridge. Then a dive-bomber attack commenced, and one bomb struck an ammunition box, setting off an explosion. The *Lexington* began to list, with several fires burning; these fires remained out of control, and with ample munitions aboard, the decision was made at 1707 hours to abandon ship. In the photograph, men wait in neat lines on the flight deck while others climb down the ropes into the water. Nearby destroyers and whaleboats clustered around the carrier in the calm waters and methodically picked up the men. Nobody was drowned or hurt in the abandonment. NARA

The USS *Lexington* is seen here with a huge plume of smoke emerging from its deck. After the ship's abandonment, another explosion racked it. With everyone off the ship, the destroyer USS *Phelps* fired its torpedoes at the carrier, dispatching it into 2,400 fathoms of water. Despite this apparent success, the Japanese navy retreated; the major ramification was that Port Moresby remained under Australian control. NARA

Australian troops help clean up the wreckage left in Darwin, Australia, after the first Japanese air raid on February 19, 1942, which lasted thirty minutes. Darwin was the administrative seat in the Northern Territories and just across the Arafura Sea and Torres Strait from Papua New Guinea. At the request of the relatively new Prime Minister Curtin, the Northern Territories of Australia were incorporated into the ABDA command zone on January 24. Darwin was also a key staging post in Allied supply routes to the East Indies. Due to a dockyard workers' strike, the harbor was crammed with ships carrying vital supplies for the Allied troops.

The attack was mounted by 188 Japanese aircraft launched from four IJN carriers 200 miles away under the command of Vice Admiral Nagumo, who led the Pearl Harbor raid. Eight ships were sunk, including the USS *Peary*, and another thirteen were damaged. Two hours later, fifty more planes from captured Dutch fields in the NEI destroyed Darwin's airfield. Over the next twenty-one months, Darwin was bombed another sixty-two times.
USAMHI

Gen. Douglas MacArthur (center), AIF CIC Gen. Thomas Blamey (left), and Prime Minister Curtin (right) meeting in Australia in late March 1942. It was Curtin who requested that Roosevelt assign MacArthur as commander of Allied Forces in the Southwest Pacific, knowing that the United States would have to bear the brunt of Australia's defense. In Melbourne, MacArthur and Curtin cemented a strong working relationship and personal liking for each other. "We two, you and I, will see this thing through together," MacArthur told Curtin. "We can do it and we will do it. You take care of the rear and I will handle the front." On March 30, it was formally decided that MacArthur, from Australia, would command the offensives to recapture the islands north of Australia, the NEI, and ultimately the Philippines. The next day MacArthur was appointed CIC of the Southwest Pacific Area Theater, effective April 18, 1942. USAMHI

General MacArthur (left) and General Blamey (far right) at the front, along the Kokoda Trail in Papua in October 1942. During the dark days of the summer of 1942, American Chief of Staff Gen. George C. Marshall wanted Australian and Dutch officers to be included on MacArthur's senior staff in Australia. Blamey was recalled from his command of Australian forces in the Middle East to become CIC of Australian Military Forces in Australia. MacArthur begrudgingly accepted Blamey but ignored him. All eleven of MacArthur's major headquarters assignments were American, including eight senior officers that their leader had brought with him from Bataan and Corregidor. During the Japanese offensive down the Kokoda Trail, which reached a crisis point in mid- to late-September, MacArthur had begun making condescending and pejorative remarks about the élan of Australian troops and their commanders fighting the Japanese. At times, Blamey was in conflict with MacArthur's egocentric will, and one day he admitted, "the best and the worst things you hear about him [MacArthur] are both true."
USAMHI

CHAPTER 2
TERRAIN

New Guinea is the second largest island in the world, at 1,500 miles long, and is located immediately north of the Australian continent. Australia's military planners regarded it as a buffer against Japanese invasion of its Northern Territories. The southeastern part, Papua, which occupies one-third of the total area, was administered by Australia.

In the almost 400 years of Portuguese, Dutch, British, German, and Australian colonial involvement on New Guinea, all that existed were a few coconut plantations, trading posts, and Christian missions, such as at Buna and Gona on the northeastern coast. New Guinea possessed no cities or towns, with the exception of the smaller ones at Port Moresby, Milne Bay, Lae, and Finschhafen. The world's second largest island was comprised of numerous small villages inhabited by native Melanesians of differing tribal origin.

Papua emanates from the Dutch meaning "fuzzy," a reference to the bushy hair of the Melanesians. There were 100,000 inhabitants representing numerous Melanesian tribes in Papua. The main town was Port Moresby, on the south coast, with a population of 3,000 before the war, comprised mostly of native Papuans.

There were just a few villages along Papua's northern coast, including Buna, Gona, Lae, and Salamaua. Away from Port Moresby, only native trails connected the north and south coasts; the most famous was to be the Kokoda Trail.

The nature of a theater's terrain lies at the heart of military tactics. Terrain features enable an experienced soldier to increase the power of a defensive position or, conversely, to select the most suitable path for an offensive. In sharp contrast is geography, which in military terms examines the relationship of one place to another in regard to distance, size, and value of the point of focus, as well as how suitable lines of communication will be. Thus, military geography serves to dictate strategic decision-making and necessitates particular logistics to achieve those plans.

Papua's interior was inhospitable, to say the least. The Owen Stanley Range of high mountains dominates the topography, and the area is replete with jungles and swamps. The geographical and climatic obstacles to conducting military operations by either side were immense in terms of troop movements, reinforcements, supply, and care of the wounded.

Jungle-covered mountain ridges near the gap in the Owen Stanley Range, as seen from an Allied aircraft in 1943. The Owen Stanley Range, over which ran the Kokoda Trail, is approximately 100 miles long and appears to have been "folded" into a series of ridges, each rising higher and higher, up to 7,000 feet, and then declining to lower ones of about 3,000 feet. NARA

An aerial view of the Kokoda Trail showing the heavily jungled mountainous terrain that the track was cut through. The fighting along the Kokoda Trail between the Australians and Japanese during the summer of 1942 was a divisional commander's war on a narrow front where tactics were dictated by local conditions and events. The terrain turned it into a slogging match. USAMHI

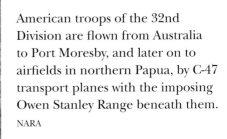

American troops of the 32nd Division are flown from Australia to Port Moresby, and later on to airfields in northern Papua, by C-47 transport planes with the imposing Owen Stanley Range beneath them. NARA

Australian soldiers struggle to carry one of their own wounded on a makeshift litter up a steep portion of the Kokoda Trail. From Port Moresby at the southern tip of Papua, the Kokoda Trail started out as a road but extended just 25 miles to Uberi, a village on a plateau in front of the main Owen Stanley Range; from there it became nightmarish even for one soldier carrying only his own gear and weapon. AWM

Australians slip ascending the endless ladder of muddy terrain, an apt description for the Kokoda Trail. The digger to the right is using a handy tool—a walking stick. From Uberi, the Kokoda Trail rose 1,200 feet in the first 3 miles along a jungle staircase with steps that varied from 10 to 18 inches in height. To prevent falling, troops often used walking sticks. After climbing 1,200 miles, the track dropped 1,600 feet before the final climb of 2,000 feet up the Imita Range, which was almost a straight vertical for the last few hundred yards. AWM

American troops of the 32nd Division make their way to Embogo from Kokoda by crossing a log bridge over the Eora Creek on November 5, 1942. Embogo was near the northern Papuan coast to the southeast of Buna. The bridge must have been hazardous to cross since fellow soldiers are standing up to their thighs in the creek to prevent any GIs from falling into it. NARA

American officers and men cross a bridge improvised from felled tree trunks on their way to the front line in Buna to avoid walking in the wet muck below the log. From Templeton's Crossing, the Kokoda Trail rose up and down again for about 10 miles to Kokoda, halfway to Buna, which had been an administrative center, and Gona, an old mission. From Kokoda to Buna, roughly 40 air miles, the country was not quite as mountainous and there was more downhill terrain for men marching farther north. However, approaching Buna and Gona the terrain, although flat, was swamp-ridden. NARA

American 32nd Division soldiers crawl on their knees in mud along the north Papuan coastline in order to feel out a Japanese position on the way to Buna in the autumn of 1942. Japanese engineers had made Buna a 10-mile-long and several miles deep fortified zone for the 7,000 IJA veterans of the Kokoda Trail. The 32nd Division approached Buna in a motley array of sea crafts that could not transport artillery. The green 32nd Division went into this Papuan swamp unprepared for jungle combat against a nearly invisible and well-fortified Japanese foe with machine-gun nests and pillboxes. What was lacking was the signature of the later U.S. Army: namely, immense artillery and air support for the infantryman. USAMHI

Tired and ragged Australian troops pass an abandoned Japanese bicycle in the thick mud of the Kokoda Trail during the summer of 1942. After advancing from Buna in July and August, the Japanese South Seas Detachment, an elite naval landing force, was stopped by the Australians at the Imita Ridge near Ioribaiwa in September, an elevation from which the Japanese could see the nocturnal searchlights of Port Moresby. Later that month, the Japanese were ordered to withdraw due to the drain of reinforcements for the Guadalcanal campaign in the Solomon Islands. On September 28, 1942, the Japanese trekked back to Buna along the Kokoda Trail with the Australians close behind. AWM

Gaunt Australian troops fighting the Japanese at Milne Bay during the summer of 1942 march through deep mud, since the rain seldom stopped during August and September. The Aussies were often afflicted with diseases, and they suffered from malnutrition, too. The climate was atrocious—humid and hot all day, but frigid at night, with almost continuous rain—making the track treacherous and a mass of slippery mud with protruding vegetation roots. Mosquitoes, mites, chiggers, and leeches were everywhere. Hookworm could be contracted by walking barefoot, so troops were strongly encouraged to wear their shoes. Other diseases in this tropical hell included malaria, dengue fever, dysentery, and jungle rot. AWM

American GIs rest on a log in the jungle as the tropical rain drenches them. Note how the two riflemen have the muzzles of their weapons covered with their hands. Another effect of the torrential downpour was malaria; plotting the incidence of malaria and inches of rainfall reveals that they were parallel. In the June–December period, the rate could be 100 cases per 1,000 soldiers each week. The troops were given quinine, which suppressed the symptoms, allowing blood donors for the wounded to pass it on unknowingly. Furthermore, the quinine came from Java, and with the Japanese conquest there, it became scarce. USAMHI

Cramped Australian soldiers on branches bridging one of the ubiquitous small streams that mired the terrain around Buna at Sanananda Point. These troops were in such close proximity to the enemy that they could hear their voices. The soldier on the left is holding his SMLE rifle, while the other is aiming his Bren light machine gun. AMW

An aerial view of the Kumasi River with its Wairopi Bridge, which in pidgin means "wire rope." The span across the waterway has been interrupted since a portion was destroyed by American air bombardment during the Japanese retreat to Buna, 30 miles to the north. The Kumasi River was a fast-running, dangerous, unpredictable watercourse with 6-foot-high banks near the bridge.

In November 1942, Maj. Gen. Tomitaro Horii was in command of the Japanese South Seas Detachment, which was then in retreat along the Kokoda Trail. He decided to make a stand near Kokoda, to the west of Wairopi, instead of pulling back to the northern Papuan coast at Buna. To the east of Kokoda, the Australians outflanked the Japanese positions at the Oivi and Gorari settlements, forcing them off the trail and into the vicinity of the Kumasi River. Although many of the Japanese infantrymen managed to slip through to Buna, Horii, hearing gunfire, decided to risk crossing the river in a canoe with his aides on November 18; however, all drowned. NARA

An American soldier crosses a muddy stream in Hollandia with the water up to his chest, using a rope-anchored native canoe to assist him. Hollandia, on the northern coast of Dutch New Guinea, was another site for the GIs to invade on April 22, 1944. They seized both vital airfields and, with simultaneous assaults at Aitape and Tanamerah Bay, dominated a 150-mile stretch of coastline, trapping roughly 60,000 Japanese troops there. NARA

An American soldier of the 32nd Division wades knee-deep in the muddy water of a swamp in the Buna sector. His right hand is wielding a machete to hack through the dense vegetation as he searches for Japanese soldiers who used this as cover to set up ambushes. NARA

An AIF 7th Infantry Division patrol marches abreast, knee-deep in a swamp, on their trek through the jungle near the Kokoda Trail on the way to Buna. Extensive areas south of both Buna and Gona were designated as "waterlogged" areas in the fighting from November 1943 to January 1944. It would ultimately require seven Australian brigades and four American regiments over two months of brutal fighting to reduce the Japanese positions in the Buna-Gona area. AWM

American troops sit atop their slit trench in Hollandia in early May 1944, brewing cocoa in a captured Japanese kettle. The entrenchment is half-filled with the ubiquitous water. USAMHI

American soldiers wade through a swamp on Noemfoor Island off the northwest coast of Dutch New Guinea in search of a downed Japanese plane to photograph. USAMHI

U.S. Marines make good use of felled tree trunks to traverse the wet terrain of Cape Gloucester on the island of New Britain. General MacArthur intentionally picked this landing site since the terrain was abysmal, precluding a pitched battle with the Japanese. Veterans of Guadalcanal complained that the water was terrible, soaking one incessantly. NARA

U.S. Army soldiers wearing helmets pass through a coconut grove at the captured Japanese village of Depapre, 30 miles from Hollandia, as mopping-up operations continued on the north coast of Dutch New Guinea in May 1944. Although tasty for their milk and meat, there was a downside to coconuts: A 5-pound nut falling 60 feet from a tree in a plantation area could kill a man not wearing a helmet. NARA

American soldiers of the 163rd Regimental Combat Team (RCT) seek cover from naval bombardment at the water's edge during their assault on Wakde Island, northwest of Hollandia, along the northern coast of Dutch New Guinea on May 17, 1944. The Japanese defenders used fierce machine-gun and mortar fire from their concealed positions. A Landing Craft Vehicle, Personnel (LCVP) is in the background. NARA

Dense vegetation surrounds and conceals GIs of the 35th Infantry Division on Vella Lavella in the Solomons as they await orders to move out. The two soldiers are holding their M1 Garand rifles. USAMHI

American soldiers of the 32nd Division at Buna occupy a former Japanese trench covered with dense foliage, their M1 Garand rifles at the ready. USAMHI

GIs at Hollandia advance cautiously through coconut trees with their full packs on and carrying extra ammunitions boxes. The soldier to the left has an M1 carbine, which was useful for jungle fighting because of its smaller size. The soldier to the right has a machete attached to his backpack to hack through the thick undergrowth. NARA

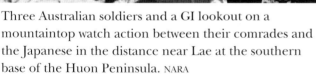

Three Australian soldiers and a GI lookout on a mountaintop watch action between their comrades and the Japanese in the distance near Lae at the southern base of the Huon Peninsula. NARA

A wounded Australian soldier gets some shade under the large leaf of a banana plant as he is tended to by a Papuan native and one of his comrades. USAMHI

American reinforcements march single-file toward Buna wearing their soft field hats. They walk on a village path adjacent to a native banana plantation in Papua. NARA

An American company-size infantry patrol emerges from tall kunai grass onto a dirt track north of the Korako Airstrip 3 miles south of Aitape in late April 1944. NARA

Australian infantrymen conceal themselves in tall kunai grass beside an M3 Stuart tank at Buna as it advances to clear out Japanese pillboxes at the edge of Semini Creek. LIBRARY OF CONGRESS

Three American soldiers patrol through tall kunai grass for stray Japanese in the captured Buna area of northern Papua. NARA

Not all terrain in the Southwest Pacific Area (SWPA) Theater was wet. Here, two GIs struggle to dig a foxhole through coral near the airstrip on Los Negros in February 1944. NARA

Unlike unit headquarters (HQ) that most theaters possessed, the 127th RCT command post is located in a jungle clearing. Col. John E. Grosse (seated) studies plans and maps for the next upcoming attack. NARA

An outdoor staff planning session of the U.S. 128th Infantry Regiment is led by Lt. Col. Alexander MacNab in a jungle clearing just outside of Warisota Plantation, 3 miles west of Embogo along the coast to the southeast of Buna. NARA

Communications are vital to any modern field force, and the jungle canopy of New Guinea could often interfere with signals. Here, an American army lieutenant receives reports of artillery on a field telephone; the telephone wire is visible running over the tops of his feet. USAMHI

Immediately upon landing at Hollandia beach in Dutch New Guinea in April 1944, signal communications were hastily established with the naval force offshore using small, compact, efficient, portable radio receivers and transmitters at the edge of a coconut grove. NARA

A U.S. Army radio crew set up their device with a very tall aerial in a small jungle clearing near Hollandia to augment the sending and receiving of signals. NARA

A 126th Infantry Regiment signal crew of the U.S. 32nd Division at Aitape on the Driniumor River communicates with an artillery spotter plane during the operation to Tadji Airfield. The crew, with their transmitter and receiver, had to be out in the open, making the members targets for enemy snipers. NARA

A telephone center that was set up two hours after the parachute drop at Kamiri Airstrip on Noemfoor Island off the coast of Dutch New Guinea in early July 1944. Notice all the telephone wires descending the hill to the right to be inserted into the portable switchboard. USAMHI

U.S. Army signalmen wade across a stream at Aitape, carrying a large spool of telephone cable in order to lay communication wires to forward positions. NARA

An Australian signalman splices together transmitter cable severed by an explosion near Port Moresby. Even a rear echelon area could have its communications disrupted by the constant threat of a Japanese air raid. USAMHI

CHAPTER 3
LOGISTICAL INNOVATIONS FOR THE TERRAIN

The Australians, Americans, and Japanese, who had conducted their lengthy military campaign on the Asian mainland in China, were not prepared for a major war in the South Pacific, which was not only remote but also disease-ridden and ubiquitously wet. The Australians, many of whom had experience in the North African desert, Greece, Crete, and Syria, had not had any training for the upland jungle they found in several parts of Papua. The battle zone across the diverse terrain of New Guinea emphasized how important it was to use it properly. In order for the combatants to advance in New Guinea, they would need to be able to construct improvised bridges and roads where water and mud governed. Because of the extensive coastline of northern Papua near Buna, troops of the American 32nd Division sailed for that destination on a motley collection of coastal craft and wooden schooners. These inadequate vessels were very vulnerable to Japanese air attack and could not carry artillery, tanks, or heavy equipment. It was no wonder U.S. Navy officers did not want to risk their larger craft in unfamiliar waters against an enemy who had control of the airfields, despite the Allies' efforts to wrest it from them.

Furthermore, both sides tried to enlist the aid of the local Melanesian native population to assist them in the movement of supplies and the wounded. The Japanese employed them in forced labor, paid them in rice and tobacco, and gave little regard to their well-being. In contrast, those employed by the Allies were administered by the Australian New Guinea Administration Unit (ANGAU), with regulations that addressed proper pay, treatment, and conditions.

The Japanese Eighteenth Army infantrymen had a reputation for being masters at jungle warfare, using camouflage and stealth. In Malaya they demonstrated an uncanny ability to leave main tracks and outflank their enemies. These same offensive tactics were employed in Papua initially, where, after circumventing Australian positions, they would emerge from the jungle and unleash devastating fire from machine guns, mortars, grenades, and lower-caliber artillery pieces. Once committed to the defensive, especially after the American 1st Marine Division was well entrenched on Guadalcanal, Japanese theater commanders for Papua ordered a halt to the Port Moresby offensive down the Kokoda Trail. The Japanese infantrymen and SNLF troops sought locations of concealment: trenches, rifle pits, coconut treetops, pillboxes, or camouflaged entrenchments. If the Japanese concealment methods were successful, the American and Australian assault troops would never see the defenders and come under withering fire; this became quite evident at both Buna and Gona in the autumn and winter of 1942–43.

All tidal swamps were home to trees with ancient root systems carrying nutrients from the water that covered the saturated ground. These root systems were so complex that they served as excellent natural machine-gun nests. The Allied attackers would learn, often on the spot, to identify likely concealed strong defensive positions and probe them. Once positions were properly identified, they would use bazookas, flamethrowers, tanks, and artillery on them; air strikes were limited since the dense jungle canopy precluded necessary bomb-strike observation. Direct infantry assaults were risky, though sometimes necessary. They were replaced by smaller infantry units going forward with covering fire from a cooperating machine-gun or rifle unit. In this manner, alternating advance and covering fire, the units would move forward against the Japanese positions.

In the early fall of 1942, the Australians pursued the retreating Japanese Special Naval Landing Detachment back up the Kokoda Trail to Buna. Here, Australians travel across the fast-flowing Kumusi River, which crosses the Kokoda Trail at Wairopi, using a device called a "flying fox" that pulled the infantryman in a rope basket. USAMHI

Australian infantrymen use a makeshift rope bridge at Wairopi to cross the Kumusi River. The original bridge was destroyed by Allied bombing raids as the Japanese retreated to Buna. USAMHI

Australian engineers and their native Papuan helpers construct a rope and wooden plank bridge across one of the innumerable waterways on their trek from Kokoda toward Buna and Gona in November 1942. USAMHI

U.S. 128th Regiment, 32nd Infantry Division soldiers between the Warisota Plantation and Boreo area in November 1942 get across a river by walking over two parallel coconut tree trunks made into a footbridge. USAMHI

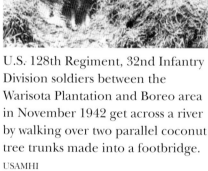

GIs of the 32nd Division cross over a log and wooden plank footbridge built by the Japanese that spans Entrance Creek to the Buna Mission sector in the late fall of 1942. NARA

Two infantrymen cross over a log-plank repair of a damaged bridge across Entrance Creek to Musita Island, which was connected to Buna Station in northern Papua. USAMHI

American soldiers of the 32nd Division cross a hastily patched-up bridge across Simeni Creek that had been damaged by Japanese artillery and machine-gun fire days before during the Buna offensive. NARA

GIs of the 32nd Infantry Division walk over a long bridge of coconut tree trunks on the way to Buna. Most wear their floppy fatigue hats and have Papuan natives assisting them. USAMHI

The versatile Willys jeep, seen here in convoy, enabled American quartermasters to bring supplies to the front line through a mud track. With the wet terrain, mud was everywhere. USAMHI

American soldiers drive their 2½-ton truck over woven mesh matting along a muddy Bougainville coconut grove path. Bougainville, located in the northwestern sector of the Solomon Islands, had several vital airfields for the Allies to capture. Note the rifle on the hood of the truck; GIs were always on the alert for Japanese snipers. USAMHI

GIs of the 37th Infantry Division on Bougainville do it the hard way, hauling 5-gallon cans of water to the front lines up the steep slopes of Hill 700. NARA

Shirtless American engineers of the 114th Engineer Battalion direct native Papuan laborers in the construction of a corduroy road during the campaign for Buna in the late fall and early winter of 1942. NARA

Vehicles of the 32nd Infantry Division drive across a steel-tracked pontoon bridge erected by the U.S. Army Engineer Corps in the Aitape area. Aitape was assaulted simultaneously with Hollandia and Tanahmerah Bay—all of which dominated a 150-mile coastal stretch of northern New Guinea—in order to entrap 60,000 Japanese troops and seize vital airfields for the continued offensive. NARA

A newly built solid wooden bridge over a New Guinea river erected by the U.S. Army Engineer Corps to support heavy vehicular traffic as the advance continued along the northern coast. NARA

U.S. Army engineers use two Caterpillar tractors in tandem to make a path and pull a trailer loaded with supplies and ammunition for an artillery piece. USAMHI

U.S. Army Engineers roll out metal matting over the thick mud of a track to create a usable road surface in a coconut grove on the northern New Guinea coast in June 1943. USAMHI

Australian and American soldiers near Lae at the base of New Guinea's Huon Peninsula move out along an emergency roadway of wooden planks topped with metal mesh matting. Countless numbers of these roads had to be constructed to get supplies to the front-line troops to sustain the Allied assault. NARA

U.S. Army Engineers use heavy metal matting to combat the mud and establish a road for a new patrol torpedo (PT) boat base on the northern coast of New Guinea. These PT boats, in conjunction with the U.S. Army Fifth Air Force, instituted an around-the-clock interdiction of Japanese navy resupply and troop reinforcement for the beleaguered Japanese troops on New Guinea. USAMHI

U.S. Army engineers begin construction of an airstrip that could accommodate bombers on Morotai Island by laying down Pierce planking on level, smoothed ground in October 1944. USAMHI

U.S. Army Engineers build an observation post in a treetop on Hill 260 to help range artillery fire against Japanese positions on Bougainville in the Solomon Island chain. NARA

U.S. Army Engineers construct a new command post out of tree trunks and earth about 100 yards away from the Japanese lines on Arawe, on the southwest end of New Britain, in January 1944. The island, situated in the Bismarck Archipelago, was home to Rabaul and its harbor and airfields. Note the GI in the left background armed with his M1 carbine guarding against the ubiquitous danger of a Japanese sniper or infiltrator. The coconut-log roof insured that only heavy artillery ordnance or an aerial bomb of sufficient weight would penetrate the command bunker. USAMHI

Due to the ever-present water along north Papua in the Buna sector, GIs bring a boatload of rations up the Girua River in collapsible assault boats in December 1942. NARA

GIs of the 128th Infantry Regiment of the 32nd Division use collapsible boats to ferry themselves across the Siwori Creek, which runs to the west of Buna Village on Papua's northern coast, in late November 1942. Note the rope guide across the waterway. NARA

Coastal shuttle operations, using canoes manned and oared by Papuan natives, deliver supplies to GIs ashore during the Buna offensive from a wooden schooner offshore. The admirals of the U.S. Navy were unwilling to commit their ships for such operations with Japanese land-based aircraft present at Buna's new and old airstrips. NARA

GIs of the 32nd Division used every available type of ship for running supplies and reinforcements for the Buna operation in late autumn 1942. Here, a wooden two-masted schooner is used. NARA

A motorized barge delivers supplies to American 32nd Division troops along the coastline during the Buna campaign of late 1942. NARA

Australian troops get ready to load one of their mountain howitzer artillery pieces onto a captured Japanese barge after dragging it along the beach near Oro Bay during the Buna operation. NARA

As the war progressed, more sophisticated landing vessels became available for use in the New Guinea theater. Here, a Landing Vehicle, Tracked (LVT), called a "Buffalo," transports GIs at the edge of Sentani Lake near Hollandia in late April 1944. The LVT's crew is firing their .50-caliber machine gun at Japanese in the brush. USAMHI

An LVT Buffalo ferries GIs along the shores of Lake Sentani near Hollandia in late April 1944 with its .50-caliber machine gunners scanning the skies for Japanese aircraft. NARA

GIs of the 41st Infantry Division sit in the DUKWs transporting them to Biak Island. The coral reef at Biak precluded the use of the larger Landing Ship, Tanks (LST) and Landing Craft, Infantry (LCI). The DUKWs were capable of traversing the coral; after landing, the DUKWs would return to the larger vessels offshore to continue the disembarkation. NARA

Papuan natives formed into a
constabulary honor guard stand at
attention as Australian major
general George A. Vasey,
commander of the AIF 7th Division,
awards native litter carriers with
medals for their gallant and
compassionate action. Decent
treatment of the Papuan natives
convinced them to work with the
Allies and not the Japanese.
LIBRARY OF CONGRESS

Native Papuan carriers at Wau in the Markham River
Valley in 1942 set out on the trek to bring supplies to
the forward areas while Australian soldiers observe
their activity. The Papuans were treated decently and
received pay from the Australians. USAMHI

Papuan natives kept going all day through steep,
trackless undergrowth, delivering supplies and
evacuating wounded from the front line to rear echelon
hospitals. LIBRARY OF CONGRESS

An outrigger canoe helps Papuan natives bring fragile boxes of plasma to forward aid stations. LIBRARY OF CONGRESS

Papuan natives cross a new temporary bridge made out of wooden planks and rope; a recent flood had washed away the previous bridge. LIBRARY OF CONGRESS

Native Papuan litter bearers carry a wounded Australian soldier across a fast-moving stream along the Kokoda Trail to a rear echelon hospital. LIBRARY OF CONGRESS

Papuan litter carriers lining up in a New Guinea coconut grove on the Buna front lines to take wounded Australian and American soldiers down the Kokoda Trail toward Port Moresby and hospital care.

Australian wounded are carried through a coconut plantation on the Buna front and then along a dirt path surrounded by tall kunai grass, headed south toward Port Moresby via the Kokoda Trail.

Young Papuan boys assist Allied troops by rolling fuel drums removed from a small boat along a beach on the northern New Guinea coast in the vicinity of Buna.

Local natives clear a field of dense vegetation with only hand tools to begin the preparatory phase to construct an airfield on Kiriwina Island in July 1943. NARA

The Japanese throughout the war were masters at using the jungle terrain to their advantage. Here, using stealth, a patrol remains essentially invisible waiting for its order to advance. Their Arisaka rifles have sword bayonets fixed since the Japanese infantrymen were instilled with the tactic to close with the enemy using the bayonet. The infantryman in the center is holding his grenade discharger, misnamed "knee mortar" by the Allies. USAMHI

A heavily camouflaged Japanese patrol moves through the New Guinea jungle. Unlike their Allied counterparts, the Japanese infantrymen tried laboriously to blend into the terrain in order to unleash unexpected withering fire on advancing Allied patrols throughout the Pacific campaign. USAMHI

Moving quietly along a jungle path, a Japanese patrol is on the march, always trying to outflank their enemy when on the offensive. Patrols would frequently leave trails and use the jungle, attempting to get behind the enemy's rear and create havoc. USAMHI

Japanese sappers hold a makeshift log footbridge on their shoulders so their infantrymen can cross one of New Guinea's innumerable jungle streams. Japanese army regiments and Special Naval Landing Detachments had an inordinate number of engineers accompany them to increase the pace of the Japanese advance when on the offensive. USAMHI

A heavily camouflaged Japanese patrol crosses a stream. Each man is carrying his complete kit that could weigh up to 60 pounds, which in the New Guinea climate was extremely enervating. USAMHI

The entrance to a Japanese pillbox on Noemfoor Island, Dutch New Guinea, in July 1944. Note how it blends in with the terrain. The log roof made the fortification impervious to rifle and mortar fire, necessitating tank and infantry assault or a direct artillery hit to reduce it. USAMHI

Japanese rifle pits and bunker entrances on Buna. To an Allied patrol advancing on it, this position would be hard to detect before they were fired on. USAMHI

Exterior view of a Japanese pillbox on Noemfoor Island in July 1944. The firing slit aperture is very thin and covered with vegetation, making it almost undetectable. The heavy log roof blends in with the terrain and protects it from everything but a direct hit. USAMHI

A GI with his Thompson .45-caliber submachine gun stands in a communication trench leading to a bunker in the Buna vicinity in December 1942. Tree fronds cover the entire structure, making the trench look like one of the many small streams running in the nearby swamps. USAMHI

Exterior view of a Japanese fortification on Noemfoor Island in Dutch New Guinea. Here, the firing aperture is somewhat wider to accommodate a heavy machine gun or small-caliber antitank gun, making it a bit more visible but just as reinforced on the roof to sustain gunfire and mortar rounds. USAMHI

An exterior view of a Japanese sunken mortar pit captured by the Allied infantry in the Buna sector. The fortification was turned into an American 4.2-inch mortar site to shell other Japanese positions. USAMHI

The interior of a Japanese bomb shelter on Noemfoor Island in July 1944, with reinforced walls and roof. The benches allow occupants to wait out an air raid. USAMHI

The rear view of a Japanese fortification with a communication trench through which the defenders could enter and leave undetected by the Allied infantry advancing in front of it. A communication trench enabled movement among more than one enemy fortification. USAMHI

An extremely well-camouflaged Japanese dugout on Noemfoor Island in Dutch New Guinea. By the time Allied forces could see it, it would be too late. USAMHI

The heavy earth and log sides and roof of this reinforced Japanese ammunition dump made it impervious to all but heavy Allied ordnance, such as a tank round or a direct heavy artillery hit. Mortars, grenades, and gunfire would be insufficient to damage this structure. USAMHI

A Japanese dugout cut out of a hillside and reinforced with a log face and roof. Allied troops would advance up the steep hill and then be confronted with fire emanating from this structure. A dead Japanese infantryman lies outside on bloodstained ground. USAMHI

The interior of a Japanese fortification on Gasmata on the southern coast of New Britain in the Bismarck Archipelago in April 1944. Note its gun platform and narrow firing slit for the barrel of the weapon. Its reinforced log construction protected it from all but the heaviest fire; however, infantry could reduce it by getting TNT, hand grenades, or flames through the firing slit, or by gaining access to it via a rear entrance. USAMHI

An American infantryman cautiously enters the rear opening of a Japanese fortification with his .45-caliber Colt automatic pistol drawn. The thick log-reinforced roof limited the ways that this enemy position could be reduced. USAMHI

An American infantryman "tries on" on a Japanese pillbox that was a recently captured machine-gun nest in the jungle of New Guinea. Its wood-reinforced structure and dense vegetation camouflage would make this a lethal position for Allied infantry. USAMHI

Two GIs stand atop the fortification that previously housed a Japanese heavy machine gun in the Buna Mission sector in early 1943. The infantryman to the right is holding the barrel of the machine gun. Note its distinctive coils for air-cooling. NARA

An American GI sitting inside a Japanese reinforced shelter for troops in the Buna sector in January 1943. Note the extensive coconut log construction. USAMHI

An American infantryman points to the slit aperture for a Japanese machine gun in a reinforced fortification atop Mount Schleuther on New Britain in March 1944. USAMHI

Australians search for dead Japanese in the ditches and "foxholes" built into the floor of a coconut plantation in the Buna sector. The Australian advance was tedious, using M3 tanks, Bren carriers, 2- and 3-inch mortars, and accompanying riflemen to overcome these stubborn nests of resistance. USAMHI

An American infantryman of the 32nd Division crawls through a Japanese communication trench near Saidor in February 1944 to demonstrate how narrow it is; this made it almost invisible to oncoming Allied infantry. A Japanese helmet rests on the edge of the trench to the right. NARA

GIs in a stooped-forward position move single file through the jungle to find a Japanese machine-gun nest concealed on the Huon Peninsula in July 1943. USAMHI

A pair of GIs rushes forward toward a Japanese position on Bougainville under enemy machine-gun fire in 1944. The infantryman on the left has an 1897 Winchester pump shotgun, while the soldier on the right carries his M1 carbine; both guns were highly suitable for close-contact jungle fighting with the lurking Japanese. USAMHI

A Marine patrol hits the ground in order to conceal itself from enemy fire coming from a Japanese pillbox in the jungle around Cape Gloucester on New Britain in 1944. The Marine in the background is already getting up to reconnoiter further. NARA

An American 124th Infantry RCT of the 31st Division has one of its .30-caliber water-cooled Browning machine-gun positions giving covering fire for a patrol reconnoitering for Japanese entrenchments on the Driniumor River. The sector, near the Tadji airfields, was the target for the Aitape assault in the summer of 1944. NARA

GIs follow a tank as it advances up a dense jungle incline on Bougainville to reduce Japanese entrenchments in May 1944. The American infantryman on the right is carrying his trusted M1 Garand rifle. USAMHI

An American infantryman crouches behind the rear of a U.S. tank's hull as tank fire is directed on Japanese fortifications on Bougainville.
USAMHI

GIs following in the wake of an M4 Sherman tank "mop up" Japanese positions on Bougainville in 1944. The infantryman in the right foreground is firing his M1 Garand rifle. All of the GIs have their bayonets fixed in the event a Japanese infantryman arises from a foxhole in the jungle floor. USAMHI

GIs take cover amid coconut tree fronds as an M4 Sherman tank advances to clear Japanese strongholds with heavy-caliber gunfire in late April 1944. NARA

An M4 Sherman tank on Biak Island fires point blank at a Japanese pillbox. This intense gunfire was often needed because the reinforced wooden-log fortifications were designed to resist small-arm and mortar fire. NARA

An American infantryman to the far right fires a bazooka rocket directly into the aperture of a Japanese jungle fortification in March 1944. USAMHI

Infantrymen of the U.S. 37th Division cautiously advance on Japanese entrenched positions on Bougainville in 1944 carrying a flamethrower, which they will use on the opening of the pillbox in the lower right background. A dead Japanese soldier lies between the patrol's point man and the soldier wielding the flamethrower. USAMHI

An American infantry patrol reduces a Japanese pillbox with flame as other soldiers use their M1 Garand rifles for suppressive fire to enable the flamethrower to get close enough. NARA

An American infantryman operates a flamethrower against a Japanese pillbox amid dense New Guinea vegetation used to conceal the enemy entrenchment. USAMHI

A GI points his .45-caliber Colt automatic pistol at the opening of a Japanese hideout dug out of a large wooden log at Aitape in the spring of 1944. When the enemy soldier refused to surrender, the American infantryman shot him. NARA

GIs at Buna have their M1 Garand rifles trained on the entrance to a camouflaged Japanese bunker. LIBRARY OF CONGRESS

Australian infantry take cover behind coconut trees in a plantation in the Buna sector in the winter of 1942. The Australian-crewed M3 Stuart tank has its 37mm gun trained on a Japanese pillbox in the background to the right as an Australian soldier cautiously advances to shoot any Japanese that may try to escape the fortification. The unit markings on the tank have been "whited out" by the military censor. NARA

A dead Japanese soldier lies outside of his metal-roofed, foliage-covered dugout. An Australian soldier with his Short Magazine Lee Enfield (SMLE) rifle stands at the ready to shoot any more enemy soldiers who refuse to surrender, as was the norm at Giropa Point near Buna. AWM

Australian soldiers strip a Japanese pillbox of its roof vegetation camouflage at Giropa Point. The face and the roof of the entrenchment are heavily reinforced with wooden logs. The shirtless Australian soldier is holding his SMLE rifle. AWM

U.S. Army engineers cautiously approach the mouth of a Japanese cave on Biak Island to throw TNT satchels into it after hand grenades had silenced Japanese gunfire from its defenders. This tactic was employed to kill Japanese who were deeply embedded within the cave. Flamethrowers were also used to incinerate the defenders who refused to surrender and were willing to resist further. NARA

A pair of U.S. Navy "Seabees" accompanying the Marine landing at Cape Gloucester on New Britain views the corpses of Japanese defenders at the rear entrance of their pillbox, which the Marines reduced. Note the sandbag and log reinforcement and heavy vegetation camouflage on the roof of the bunker. NARA

A dead Japanese soldier lies at the base of a coconut tree from which he sniped at Australian troops during the Gona battle. His Arisaka rifle is draped across his left leg. USAMHI

This Japanese soldier was killed by a mortar round on Hill 225, which was adjacent to the Maffin Airstrip on Wakde Island, at the end of May 1944. His helmet and kit lie scattered around him. USAMHI

A Japanese sniper lies dead on the jungle floor. He was shot out of his coconut tree by Australian infantry in the Giropa Plantation near Buna in the early winter of 1942. USAMHI

CHAPTER 4
MILITARY LEADERS IN THE NEW GUINEA CAMPAIGN

President Roosevelt had decided to order MacArthur to leave the Philippines on March 11, 1942. With seventeen of his staff officers (the "Bataan Gang") and his family, MacArthur took a hazardous PT boat journey to Mindanao and then Army B-17 bombers to Darwin, Australia, followed by a train to Melbourne. There, he was appointed Commander of the Southwest Pacific Area (SWPA) Theater by General Marshall at the direct request of the Australian government. Prime Minister Curtin selected Gen. Sir Thomas Blamey as Allied Land Forces commander. MacArthur and his staff derided Blamey, although he had served gallantly in World War I. After being the police chief in Melbourne, he served in North Africa and the Levant with the Australian divisions there.

With the nascent corps training in Australia, comprised of the 32nd and 41st Divisions, MacArthur needed a corps commander. Marshall fortuitously sent him Lt. Gen. Robert L. Eichelberger, a West Point graduate in the Class of 1909 that included both American 32nd and 41st Infantry Division commanders: Major Generals Edwin Harding and Horace Fuller, respectively. Eichelberger's career included service in Siberia after World War I and attendance at the Command and General Staff School in 1926. He knew MacArthur in 1935 when he was secretary of the general staff. After he served as assistant division commander of the 3rd Infantry Division, Marshall appointed him superintendent of West Point in October 1940, following in the footsteps of both Robert E. Lee and Douglas A. MacArthur. After the war erupted, Eichelberger trained the 77th Infantry Division, and as a reward was given command of I Corps for the North African invasion. However, a more pressing need emanated from Australia and New Guinea, so the new lieutenant general took his I Corps staff with him to the Antipodes.

On September 10, 1942, MacArthur ordered Eichelberger's I Corps HQ to deploy Harding's 32nd Division to New Guinea to ease the burden on the Australians retreating down the Kokoda Trail to the Imita Ridge near Templeton's Crossing, about 30 miles from Port Moresby. The division was unprepared for combat, but the 126th Infantry Regiment was rushed to Port Moresby by boat. Furthermore, because of transport deficiencies, Harding's four battalions of

divisional artillery (forty-eight field guns) were left in Australia. With the Japanese retreating up the Kokoda Trail because supplies and reinforcements were diverted by Lt. Gen. Haruyoshi Hyakutake, commander of Japan's Seventeenth Army, to start a counteroffensive against the 1st U.S. Marine Division on Guadalcanal, the 32nd Division was ordered to capture the 11-mile-long group of Japanese installations at Buna on Papua's northern coast. After some bitter fighting there, MacArthur's chief of staff, Lt. Gen. Richard K. Sutherland, visited Harding on the Buna front and decided that a change in leadership was required. MacArthur ordered Eichelberger to embark to Buna on December 1, 1942, and to take over for Harding and capture the Japanese installations there. After capturing Buna—and the American press—Eichelberger was relegated back to I Corps to retrain and refit the American 32nd and 41st Infantry Divisions for future operations in New Guinea. Also, MacArthur wanted a field commander loyal to him and not to Marshall, as Eichelberger, the chief of staff's protégé was deemed to be.

MacArthur requested U.S. Third Army Commander Lt. Gen. Walter Krueger be sent to New Guinea, anticipating that he would command an army that would liberate the Philippines. MacArthur did not want American troops put under the control of Blamey as the Allied Land Forces commander. As a deception, MacArthur created Alamo Force, a task force that could remain solely under American control. When MacArthur activated Krueger's new Sixth Army as Alamo Force, Blamey would have no operational control over this expanding American force. However, for much of the remainder of 1943, MacArthur would have only Australian troops to do the fighting on New Guinea's northern coast.

Maj. Gen. George C. Kenney was dispatched to MacArthur in the summer of 1942, when the Japanese capture of Port Moresby was a likely possibility. Kenney took over the Fifth Air Force and turned it into a multidimensional unit to include troop transport and supply, aerial artillery for troops who lacked field artillery, and—with innovations perfected by his B-25 and A-20 medium bombers—the daytime interdiction of Japanese coastal shipping to their New Guinea garrisons.

Rear Adm. Daniel E. Barbey joined the MacArthur team in January 1943 to develop and implement a new naval unit, the Seventh Amphibious Force, which was charged with landing American and Australian troops on hostile shores to wrest control of those far-off places from the Japanese.

MacArthur expected the utmost loyalty from his subordinate generals and admirals. This created intense friction between the higher commands, especially when MacArthur's staff officers, formerly of Bataan and Corregidor, meddled in tactical and combat decisions.

Gen. Sir Thomas Blamey (center), commander of the Australian Armed Forces and at the time serving under MacArthur as commander of Allied Land Forces, inspects the Papuan front and meets with American regimental and Australian brigade commanders. There was an undercurrent of tension between MacArthur and Blamey, with each harboring doubts about the fighting qualities of the other's troops as the battles around Buna reached a stalemate. AWM

MacArthur (foreground) rides in a jeep past Australian troops on the way to the front lines in Papua. MacArthur was disdainful of their fighting style even though 7,000 of their compatriots had stopped a Japanese invasion at Milne Bay in August 1942, and by the end of September 1942, other Australian troops had held the Japanese from further advancing down the Kokoda Trail at Imita Ridge near Ioribaiwa. USAMHI

MacArthur (right) and Gen. George C. Kenney (left), commanding officer of the U.S. Fifth Air Force and then Allied Air Forces, Southwest Pacific Area, discussing strategy. Kenney was an innovative leader; by altering air interdiction tactics, he prevented daytime supply and reinforcement of Japan's northern New Guinea garrisons. His aircraft were pivotal in providing tactical air support for advancing American and Australian ground troops. USAMHI

From left to right, Australian minister for the army F. M. Forde, MacArthur, Blamey, and Kenney, among others, in October 1942. There had been a recent Australian victory at Milne Bay, as well as an Australian halt to the land offensive of Japanese general Tomitaro Horii's South Seas Detachment to capture Port Moresby over the Owen Stanley Range. USAMHI

From left to right, Lt. Gen. Walter Krueger, commanding general of the U.S. Sixth Army; MacArthur; Captain Cory, USN; and Vice Adm. Thomas C. Kincaid, who served as commander of MacArthur's Naval Forces Southwest Pacific (designated the U.S. 7th Fleet). MacArthur and Krueger had just returned from the Hollandia assault front on April 22, 1944. USAMHI

General MacArthur talks with U.S. Navy Capt. Herman Adolf Spanagel, commander of the USS *Nashville* from September 30, 1942, to April 25, 1944, while visiting his amphibious forces at their rendezvous spot on April 20, 1944, for the combined Hollandia, Aitape, and Tanahmerah Bay landings along the northern coast of New Guinea. The landings were to occur simultaneously in forty-eight hours. USAMHI

MacArthur tours the landing area at the newly captured Tanahmerah Bay. Krueger (left), commanding U.S. Sixth Army, and Maj. Gen. Fred I. Irving (right), commanding the 24th U.S. Infantry Division, walk behind him. NARA

Lt. Gen. Richard K. Sutherland (right), MacArthur's chief of staff SWPA, who accompanied his commander from Corregidor to Australia in March 1942 with other members of the "Bataan Gang." He is greeted by Maj. Gen. Charles P. Hill (left) and Maj. Gen. William H. Gill (center) in New Guinea. NARA

Lieutenant General Eichelberger (rear of jeep) and General Blamey (center) tour the Buna sector of northern Papua during the heavy fighting in the late winter of 1943. Eichelberger, who was training the U.S. 41st Infantry Division in Australia, was ordered to the front to take command of the U.S. 32nd Infantry Division from Maj. Gen. Edwin Harding, with the famous directive from MacArthur, "Go out there, Bob, and take Buna or don't come back alive," as he left Port Moresby for the front lines. USAMHI

Eichelberger, now commanding the U.S. 32nd Infantry Division at Buna, discusses plans for an attack on Buna Station with Col. John E. Grose, commanding that division's 127th RCT. Eichelberger took command at a time when things were looking up for the Americans before Buna. Completion of an airstrip at Dobodura near the northern New Guinea coast greatly improved the supply situation. He was also promised tank support and reinforcements. Nevertheless, when an all-out frontal assault in early December was stopped with heavy casualties, Eichelberger abandoned any more frontal attacks and waited for his promised armored support. USAMHI

Eichelberger and his escorting GIs tour some of the Buna battlefield in the newly taken Triangle area, just south of Giropa Point and Buna Mission, where the Japanese garrison HQ was situated. By mid-December, long-awaited Australian-crewed M3 Stuart light tanks arrived to reinforce the eastern flank of the Allied advance at Buna.
NARA

Lieutenant General Eichelberger (left) and Rear Adm. Daniel E. Barbey (far right), commanding the Amphibious Force at Hollandia. To the right of Eichelberger is Major General Irving, commander of the U.S. 24th Infantry Division.
NARA

Adm. William F. Halsey, Jr. (center), commander, South Pacific Force and South Pacific Area. He led American Navy and Marine forces to victory in the Solomon Islands campaign, beginning with the victory at Guadalcanal in later 1942. Here, he stands on the island of Bougainville in November 1943 talking to Maj. Gen. Roy S. Geiger, USMC (left), commanding general on the island, and Brig. Gen. Leo N. Kreber. NARA

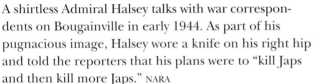

A shirtless Admiral Halsey talks with correspondents on Bougainville in early 1944. As part of his pugnacious image, Halsey wore a knife on his right hip and told the reporters that his plans were to "kill Japs and then kill more Japs." NARA

Standing under a B-17 fuselage at an Allied airfield in New Guinea, Lieutenant General Kenney (right), CIC Allied Air Forces, SWPA, chats with his deputy, Maj. Gen. Ennis C. Whitehead, prior to returning to Australia. Kenney worked so effectively as MacArthur's right hand that the SWPA Theater became an almost classic, textbook case demonstrating the effectiveness of limited air power projected over vast distances. Kenney was a great innovator in both aerial tactics and novel weaponry to destroy both the Japanese air forces and interdict naval supply and reinforcement. One of his favorite expressions was "Hell, let's try it." NARA

Capable and loyal MacArthur subordinate commanders, Lieutenant General Krueger (left) and Vice Adm. Thomas C. Kinkaid, commander of the U.S. Navy's 7th Fleet in the SWPA Theater in October 1944. MacArthur established Alamo Force—which was Krueger and his Sixth Army HQ thinly disguised—as a transparent measure to circumvent the authority of General Blamey as commander of Allied Land Forces. Although MacArthur was an Allied commander, no major staff position of his was held by an Australian officer. USAMHI

At Aitape, Lieutenant General Krueger (right) confers with Australian Air Commodore Frederick R. Scherger, RAAF (left), at the recently captured Tadji Airfield. NARA

Krueger (left) and Maj. Gen. Horace Fuller, commander of the U.S. 41st Infantry Division, inspect defenses at Hollandia after its successful amphibious assault. NARA

Lt. Gen. Alexander A. Vandergrift, USMC, commanded the Bougainville ground forces during the invasion until Maj. Gen. Roy C. Geiger, USMC, arrived. Both Marine officers were on Guadalcanal, where their leadership contributed greatly to the defense of the Marine perimeter from August to November 1942. Vandergrift was the commanding officer of the 1st Marine Division that achieved iconic status there due to its gallantry and tenacious defense of the island's airstrip, Henderson Field. NARA

The 3rd Marine Division landed at Empress Augusta Bay on Bougainville in November 1943 to avoid major Japanese resistance and was joined by several other U.S. Army units, including the 37th Infantry Division. Here, Vandergrift (second from right) talks to Commodore E. J. Moran, USN (far left), Maj. Gen. O. W. Griswold, 14th Corps Commander, and Gen. Ralph Mitchell, USMC (far right), beside a transport plane. USAMHI

Lt. Gen. Hatazo Adachi, commanded the Japanese Eighteenth Army in eastern New Guinea from November 1942 until the war ended. At its peak, Adachi commanded 80,000–90,000 men, with reinforcements of about 60,000 available within three weeks. The Japanese had about 320 operational aircraft, with another 270 ready to be flown in within 48 hours. Adachi held out in the jungle with remnants of his army until September 1945, when he learned from a radio broadcast that the emperor had surrendered. USAMHI

Adachi steps off of a transport plane upon his arrival at Wewak, the HQ for the IJA's Eighteenth Army in Eastern New Guinea, to surrender his sword to Australian officers in September 1945. He was tried for war crimes in Rabaul but committed *hara-kiri*, a ritual suicide for Japanese warriors following the *bushido* code, in September 1947. USAMHI

Lt. Gen. Haruyoshi Hyakutake, commander of Japan's Seventeenth Army, simultaneously directed the Papuan and Guadalcanal campaigns; however, he needed to deprive his South Seas Detachment on the Owen Stanley Range of vital supplies and reinforcements in order to strengthen his counterattacks on Guadalcanal. Despite having sent warships, planes, and troops, he lost both battles, necessitating the Japanese in Papua to bunker themselves in the Buna and Gona strongholds. NARA

CHAPTER 5

AMERICAN ASSAULT ON BUNA

There were two U.S. Army divisions available to MacArthur in the late summer of 1942. Maj. Gen. Edwin Harding's 32nd Division was a National Guard unit from Michigan and Wisconsin that was deployed early to Australia, missing the training that the Army Ground Forces were acquiring stateside. The other available division was the 41st, commanded by Maj. Gen. Horace Fuller, a classmate of Harding's at the United States Military Academy; however, it was still in training in Australia. In early September, MacArthur deployed the 32nd Division to Port Moresby since it was uncertain if the Australians would be able to hold against the Japanese, who were about 30 miles from that southern Papuan locale. Unfortunately, Lt. Gen. Robert Eichelberger, commanding I Corps HQ, which was responsible for training the two American divisions, was skeptical of the 32nd Division's upcoming combat role.

Buna consisted of an Australian government station called Buna Mission, a small settlement 500 yards away called Buna Village, and an airstrip. As the Australians were fighting the retreating Japanese back up the Kokoda Trail, MacArthur committed the relatively green 32nd Infantry Division to the attack on Buna. Major General Harding was a protégé of the Army Chief of Staff, Gen. George C. Marshall. Harding served with Marshall in China and was an instructor under him at the Fort Benning Infantry School.

An Australian report after the capture of Gona recalled just how well the Japanese engineers had prepared the defenses along the 11-mile front on the northern Papuan coastline that extended from Gona in the west to Cape Endaiadere to the east of Buna Mission and Giropa Point. Hundreds of coconut log bunkers lay along the stretch, some reinforced with iron plates, others with iron rails and oil drums filled with sand. In areas that were too wet for trenches and dugouts, bunkers were built 7 to 8 feet above the surface and then concealed with earth, tree fronds, and other vegetation to blend in with the terrain, making them essentially invisible. The bunkers, which could each contain from three to five machine guns, provided an intense interlocking field of fire on any advancing Allied troops. The bunkers were protected by infantry in open rifle pits located to the front, sides, and rear of the fortified entrenchments. Some infantry were hidden in foxholes in the ground, under trees, or even in hollowed-out logs, while others simply waited in the jungle where they were heavily camouflaged. Snipers in the tall coconut trees or in concealed terrain positions were a major menace in this Japanese defensive network in both the American and Australian zones.

The plan envisioned by Allied HQ was for a general advance to commence on November 16, 1942, by the Australian 7th Division and the U.S. 32nd Division against the Buna-Gona beachhead. The dividing line between the Australian and U.S. troops was to be the Girua River. While its 127th Regiment remained at Port Moresby, the rest of the 32nd Division began its assault without much of its divisional artillery since there were no ships that the U.S. Navy wanted to risk sending into the northern Papuan waters. The 2nd Battalion of the 126th Infantry Regiment assaulted Buna overland via the Kapa Kapa Trail and sustained horrific casualties from combat losses and disease. The remaining battalions of the 126th Regiment and the entire 128th Regiment were airlifted by General Kenney's Fifth Air Force. In 1942 this was a revolutionary tactic as Papuans and Army engineers began building airfields in northern Papua, notably at Dobodura, located south of Buna and east of the unfordable Girua River.

At Buna, there were more than 100 bunkers and pillboxes built by the Japanese. The American 105mm howitzer was a great "bunker buster"; however, the absence of shipping and the terrain necessitated using mortars. Even the 81mm mortar could not destroy bunkers since the delayed-action fuse had not been employed yet. By the end of November, victory was still elusive to the men of Harding's 32nd Division. With much of his division destroyed, Harding formed two large task forces out of his surviving 3,500 combat troops. Warren Force was the larger of the two and was ordered to attack the Cape Endaiadere end of the Japanese-fortified 11-mile beachhead. The smaller Urbana Force was charged with an assault on Buna village and, after taking it, an advance on to Buna Mission. MacArthur, disheartened by Harding's performance and combat troop organization, sent in General Eichelberger to replace his former West Point classmate and fellow Marshall acolyte. Logistical hurdles were overcome as 105mm howitzers were slowly flown in to the Buna front by Kenney's B-17s, and Australian-crewed M3 Stuart light tanks reached Eichelberger by the middle of December. Eventually, the Japanese entrenchments were destroyed by artillery and the tanks' 37mm guns aimed at the bunker apertures; however, it would not be until January 22 that the battle for the Buna-Gona-Sanananda beachhead was wrested from the Japanese by American and Australian infantry, armor, and air forces.

After three months of frontal assaults—since the Papuan terrain prevented envelopments with large forces—the staging base and airstrip at Buna was in Allied hands and the Japanese were forced out of Gona. The cost was staggering for both sides, with 8,500 Allied deaths (5,700 Australian and 2,800 American) and roughly 13,000 Japanese fatalities. Malaria produced 27,000 medical casualties, largely because of the shortage of quinine, which was produced mainly in Japanese-held Indonesia. As for unit integrity, the Australian 7th and American 32nd Infantry Divisions were severely mauled, while the Australian 5th and American 41st Infantry Divisions were exhausted as well. The American infantry divisions required six to twelve months of reinforcements and refitting to prepare for the next series of battles, while the Australians defended against further Japanese advances, despite the Australians' staggering losses for the total number of troops committed.

American troops of the 127th Infantry Regiment of the 32nd Division reach Port Moresby on September 17, 1942, via a coastal schooner as Australian soldiers and native Papuans look on. General MacArthur was concerned that the Japanese South Seas Detachment heading south down the Kokoda Trail would overwhelm the Australians holding them off. NARA

American troops from the 32nd Infantry Division shoulder their duffel bags and leave the deck of a Liberty ship (background) that transported them from Australia to Port Moresby in September 1942 as events looked bleak for the Australian defense of the Kokoda Trail. NARA

Battle-bound GIs board a C-47 transport carrying full equipment for jungle fighting. The complete movement and air supply was a major factor in the Allied success in Papua and a tremendous tactical innovation by Gen. George Kenney's Fifth Air Force. NARA

GIs climb into a truck to ride up to the Buna front in northern Papua after landing in Port Moresby via C-47 transport in early January 1943. NARA

After flying over swamps and jungles, these GIs disembark from a C-47 transport en route to battle the Japanese in northern Papua. A two-day march lay ahead of them to reach the front lines at Buna. Several Australian soldiers monitor their progress at this makeshift airfield. NARA

Elements of the 126th Infantry Regiment of the 32nd Division pass through the coastal village of Hariko, well to the southeast of Buna, as they head to the front lines. One battalion of this regiment traveled overland through the jungle toward Buna along the north–south running Kapa Kapa Trail and was almost destroyed in the process. NARA

GIs march through the swamps of northern Papua on the way to combat the Japanese, who had entrenched themselves in bunkers and pillboxes around Buna. USAMHI

American troops in a jeep cross a river on a log corduroy bridge on the Kapa Kapa Trail in September 1942. This was the inland route for one battalion from the 126th Infantry Regiment of the 32nd Division as it traveled through the jungle toward Buna. NARA

Lt. Col. Alexander MacNab (right), executive officer of the 128th Infantry Regiment of the U.S. 32nd Division, pauses with two of his men along a trail toward the Buna front. Native Papuan guides and bearers accompany them. NARA

Members of the 3rd Battalion and Regimental HQ of the 126th Infantry Regiment of the 32nd Division rest on a jungle trail between Boreo and Dobodura during the early phase of the campaign for Buna. Papuan guides and bearers sit in the foreground and far right. NARA

Brig. Gen. Hanford MacNider (center, seated), commander of Warren Force, goes over map coordinates for his plan to take Buna in mid-November 1942, just days before the battle started. MacNider was wounded and subsequently replaced with Col. Clarence Martin, who on December 5 assaulted Japanese positions with recently arrived Bren carriers; however, it was a complete and costly failure. NARA

Brig. Albert W. Waldron (center), the 32nd Division's artillery commander who was put in charge of the division after General Harding was fired, discusses the impending Buna battle with his subordinates on November 15, 1942. Waldron suggested that a B-17 could carry a disassembled 105mm artillery howitzer, and General Kenney made it happen. The result was that the howitzer fired off its allotment of fifty rounds, destroying six Japanese bunkers. Waldron led from the front and paid the price of leadership with a serious wound that kept him recovering for most of the war. NARA

Company M of the 128th Infantry passes through Simeni Village on its way to an advanced position near Buna. The maintenance of the 127th Infantry Regiment in Port Moresby irritated the early commanders of the Buna assault, and they clamored for these troops to be released to the front. NARA

Men of the 2nd Battalion of the 32nd Division's 128th Infantry Regiment cook breakfast at the beach near Embogo, well to the southeast of Buna along the coast. This regiment, part of Warren Force, was to march along the coastal trail and take Cape Endaiadere in the immediate vicinity of the two airfields: the Old Strip (the original Buna Station airstrip) and the New Strip (built by the Japanese). NARA

Men of the 32nd Division's 128th Infantry Regiment form a "chow line" along a muddy trail. This regiment's advance was on axes; one was the coastal trail, while a second was an inland trek that ran between the New and Old Strips. This inland trail emanated from Dobodura, where General Kenney was building an airfield. The targets of both trails were the New and Old Strips and Cape Endaiadere. NARA

An American 3-inch antiaircraft artillery (AAA) crew mans their gun at a new fighter strip at Dobodura in early 1943. This airfield, built at the urging of General Kenney, provided a proximate point to ferry in supplies and reinforcements with C-47s as well as a base for fighters, which served as "aerial artillery" since the 32nd Division lacked heavy ordnance. NARA

Lt. Col. Herbert Smith leads troops across a river on the way to Embogo along Warren Force's coastal route to Buna in November 1942. The tortuous rivers and creeks on the island often had to be crossed more than once. NARA

A platoon of American soldiers crosses over a riverbed in search of Japanese in the Buna sector. Papuan native porters and guides accompany them. NARA

An American Signal Corps soldier advances along a previous Japanese rifle pit under heavy fire in the advance to Buna. Some of his fellow soldiers stand observant for the lurking enemy while another communicates on his field telephone. NARA

An American patrol from the 1st Battalion, 128th Infantry Regiment, mans its .30-caliber Browning machine gun on the Embogo River as the Warren Force moves up the coastal trail to Buna in November 1942. NARA

A .30-caliber Browning machine-gun three-man crew aims their weapon across the river at Giruwa Point in support of the Allied advance against Sanananda Point between Buna and Gona in late 1942. The soldiers erected an improvised log breastwork to protect themselves. NARA

Across a waterway from Buna Mission, the crew of a 37mm antitank gun of the 128th Infantry Regiment fires at Japanese pillboxes tenaciously defending their position. It took artillery, aerial attack, direct tank fire, flame, and TNT satchels to destroy such fortifications. USAMHI

An American soldier, part of a 37mm antitank gun crew, looks through the opening of his camouflaged bunker at Japanese positions in Buna. In order for an antitank weapon to destroy an enemy bunker, it had to go straight through the Japanese firing slit. NARA

An American patrol crosses one of the innumerable waterways in the Buna sector with their M1 Garand rifles at the ready in the event of a Japanese ambush or snipers. A two-man .30-caliber Browning machine gun with a box of ammunition already loaded covers their crossing from the near shore in the foreground. NARA

American soldiers from the 32nd
Infantry Division examine a
captured Japanese antitank gun in a
bombproof shelter near Buna
Mission on December 26, 1942.
USAMHI

An 81mm M1 mortar crew fires in
support of infantry moving on Buna
Mission. These weapons were
unable to destroy a reinforced
Japanese bunker, and artillery was
scarce in northern Papua due to
terrain and supply issues. NARA

An American 81mm M1 mortar fires from a concealed
firing pit deep in the Buna sector jungle. Despite the
foliage concealing it, the plume of smoke emitted after
the round was fired would often identify the position.
USAMHI

A two-man mortar crew fires a 60mm M2 mortar from open terrain against Japanese positions at Buna Mission in early 1943. NARA

Warren Force, comprised of the 128th Infantry Regiment, attacked through this devastated swamp area east of the bridge between the New and Old Strips inland from Cape Endaiadere in early December 1942. NARA

Exhausted troops of the 128th Infantry Regiment march leisurely along the beach after the attack and capture of Cape Endaiadere on December 22, 1942. NARA

Two wounded American soldiers help each other in the northern Papuan jungle in the vicinity of Buna Mission. The GI on the left holds his Thompson .45-caliber submachine gun with a drum magazine while the other soldier has an M1 Garand .30-06 caliber rifle slung over his left shoulder. Both weapons had tremendous "stopping power," given the caliber of the bullet used. NARA

Two medics check on American wounded soldiers lying on makeshift wooden litters awaiting native Papuan litter bearers to carry them to Allied airfields for evacuation to Port Moresby. NARA

A U.S. jeep crewed by both Americans and Australians serves as an ambulance and transports Allied wounded to rear echelon areas from a Buna sector forward aid station. NARA

A wounded American soldier is lifted by Australians from the C-47 that transported him out of the Buna sector to a landing strip near Port Moresby. He is pulling the blanket up to shield his eyes from the sunlight. NARA

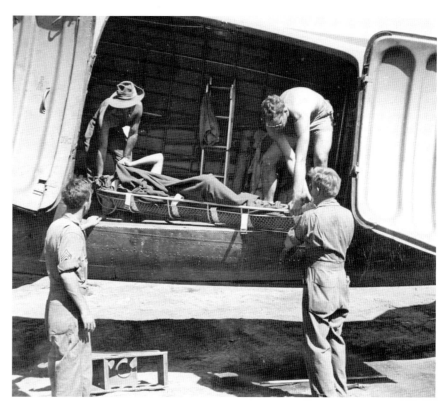

Japanese dead on the Buna Mission beach near their shattered landing barge, or *Daihatsu*, as the Allies continued final mopping-up operations in the sector. LIBRARY OF CONGRESS

Buna Mission's devastated countryside after almost three months of fighting. Very few trees remained standing and the native huts were destroyed. USAMHI

Dobodura Airstrip, built by Allied forces with the assistance of Papuan natives, where elements of the 41st Division arrived from Port Moresby in February 1943 after extensive training in Australia and acclimatization in southern Papua. NARA

Disheveled soldiers of the U.S. 32nd Infantry Division examine Japanese booty they acquired after capturing Buna Mission in late January 1943. They had suffered three months of unimaginable frontal attacks, urged on by MacArthur, in addition to the ravages of tropical diseases and malnutrition. NARA

CHAPTER 6
AUSTRALIAN CAMPAIGNS IN NEW GUINEA

After the repulse of an amphibious assault on Port Moresby in early May, an overland attempt was launched on July 22 when IJA troops of the Yokoyama Advance Force landed at Gona on the north coast. The enemy still hoped to conquer Papua.

General MacArthur had no interest in Eastern New Guinea since he could not envision it on the path back to the Philippines. However, he did correctly reason that if he held Milne Bay at the eastern end of New Guinea, he could control it with air power stationed at a newly constructed airfield there. MacArthur's engineers also scouted Buna as a possible site for an airfield; after concluding that it was, they left. However, the Japanese arrived at Buna with the same intent. With an airfield at Buna (both Old and New Strips), the Japanese thought they could go overland to seize Port Moresby. After occupying Buna, they next pushed down a nearby native track, the Kokoda Trail, over the Owen Stanley Mountain range, as the route to seize Port Moresby, in an analogous fashion to Singapore. The trail was a 145-mile mud path that crossed some of the most inhospitable terrain in the world. Thus began the brutal confrontation for the Kokoda Trail—lasting well into September—which committed the remainder of the IJA's 144th Infantry Regiment along with the South Seas Detachment HQ (Gen. Tomitaro Horii's 4,400 troops that had captured Rabaul) and elements of the IJA's 41st Infantry Regiment (2,100 troops), under Col. Yazawa Kiyomi.

The Australians halted the advance of the Japanese 27 air miles from Port Moresby near Ioribaiwa at Imita Ridge in mid-September. The Japanese supply system was stretched to its limits, and the offensive had resulted in 80 percent killed, wounded, and disabled by disease. General Horii halted the Japanese offensive to Port Moresby and was ready to prepare defensive works and await reinforcements. However, the Imperial Japanese High Command ordered him to withdraw back on the Kokoda Trail on September 24 and establish a defensive position at Buna and Gona on the northern coast. These faraway sites would be the scene of horrific jungle fighting by American and Australian forces that would last into January 1943. This was a strategic retreat because of an increasing need for troop reinforcements elsewhere. At the end of September, the IJA was ordered to redirect their efforts at reclaiming Guadalcanal from the American 1st Marine Division that had landed there and at Tulagi on August 7, 1942.

One last offensive was conducted in late August 1942. The IJN's 8th Fleet sent a force to seize Milne Bay on the southeast end of Papua to provide an airfield and base to support the ongoing Port Moresby assault and concurrent Guadalcanal operation. MacArthur had the idea earlier and in July sent thousands of Australian troops to seize a stretch of shoreline at Milne Bay so U.S. Army and Australian engineers could build an airfield there. The 2,000-man Hayashi Force (1st Landing Force) launched from New Ireland and landed on the bay's northern shore on the night of August 25. The Australians, with some Americans, possessed numerical superiority and defeated the mixed SNLF troops; the survivors were evacuated on September 4–5.

As the crisis on the Kokoda Trail had passed, Gen. Sir Thomas Blamey demanded that the Allied offensive toward Papua's northern coast was to belong to the Australians. Having initially been overwhelmed by the Japanese just weeks before, he reasoned it was the right place for the diggers to win back their fighting reputation. There were at least 4,000 Japanese at Gona and approximately 2,500 at Buna. These Japanese troops were well protected against any attack from inland. Swamps and dense jungle channeled the Allied attackers down a handful of trails, where a Japanese machine gun in a reinforced pillbox could hold off a battalion. With the Americans advancing along the northern New Guinea coast, the Australians would expend much blood to wrest control of both Buna and Gona from the Japanese.

After Buna and Gona, the Australians continued in the Allied offensive on the Huon Peninsula at Lae, Salamaua, Finschhafen, and in the Markham River Valley. The combat was fierce, but the Australian reputation for being tough fighters was evident at all sites, even if American influence as the dominant partner was taking hold. The Huon Peninsula and Markham River Valley are probably the most daunting, if not most malignant, military terrains in the South Pacific. On September 4, 1943, Australian troops landed near Lae, the first step in Blamey's New Guinea Force to clear the Huon Peninsula. After capturing Lae, the

Australian 7th Division advanced west into the upper Ramu Valley to secure airfields for Kenney's Fifth Air Force. The Australian 9th Division landed at Finschhafen and, against strong opposition at Sattelberg, eventually cleared the western shore of the Vitiaz Strait.

The Australians campaigned in a quadrant enclosed by the coastal village of Salamaua, westward to the inland mining settlement of Wau, and then northwest to the harbor town of Madang. This area included the Huon Peninsula, the mountains surrounding Wau, and the malaria-ridden Bulolo Valley, about 150 miles west-northwest of Buna. Along the coast was the forbidding Finisterre Range, which was rugged, steep, and covered with dense rain forest. It rained heavily there almost every day, making living conditions miserable. There was an ongoing constant battle with mud, slush, rain, and cold.

The Japanese had built up the prewar airfield and harbor at Lae in Northeast New Guinea into a major base and anchorage on the Huon Peninsula. The Japanese could land at Lae and then advance to Wau with the intent of attacking Port Moresby again along a different geographic axis. However, the Allied air forces prevented Japanese reinforcements, and a combined Allied offensive finally overcame the enemy bastion at Lae. The Americans pushed along the coast while the Australians advanced on a western axis from Wau through the Markham Valley. Japanese losses in their prolonged defense of Salamaua against the American and Australian advances left Lae exposed to an Allied envelopment. In early September 1943, almost 8,000 Australian troops were landed 18 miles east of Lae, in the rear of the Japanese defenses.

Japanese light Type 95 Ha-Go tanks—which were essentially two-man machine-gun platforms disabled during the abortive Milne Bay offensive of late August 1942—are inspected by Australian troops in September 1942. AWM

An Australian infantry section marches single file past the disabled Japanese light Type 95 Ha-Go tanks in September. The heavily outnumbered Japanese at Milne Bay stood no chance against the Australians, many of whom were veterans of the North African desert campaigns. AWM

A disabled Japanese landing barge, or *Daihatsu*, washes up on the beach at Milne Bay after the Japanese 2,000-man Hayashi Force (1st Landing Force) failed to seize the area on August 25, 1942. More than half of the landing force was killed or wounded, and the Japanese pulled out ten days after landing. The *Daihatsu* was usually armed with two light machine guns and could carry 100–120 men, an artillery piece, and a light tank or truck. AWM

An Australian patrol near Milne Bay spots a dead Japanese soldier in the brush after the failed landing at the very eastern tip of Papua in August–September 1942. NARA

Australian soldiers using picks, shovels, and the occasional pneumatic drill construct a road up a steep hill with Milne Bay in the background. Australian and U.S. forces arrived at Milne Bay a month before the Japanese, and with a numerical advantage of about five to one, they overwhelmed the enemy landing force for their first victory in Papua. NARA

Australian militia and native carriers stop at Eora Creek Village for a well-earned rest on their way out of a forward area along the Kokoda Trail after combating the Japanese advance from Buna over the Owen Stanley Range. The enemy attempted to seize Port Moresby from behind since the strategic defeat at the Battle of the Coral Sea precluded an amphibious landing there. USAMHI

An Australian militiaman wounded at Oivi is taken back down the Kokoda Trail to a rear echelon dressing station. Oivi was located just to the east of the village of Kokoda, and the Australian militia was defeated there at the end of August 1942. LIBRARY OF CONGRESS

The Australian Militia Imperial Force's 39th Battalion stands at parade at Menari in late September 1942 after having engaged the Japanese on the Kokoda Trail throughout the summer months. This unit was wracked with disease and incurred so many casualties that it almost ceased being active. Note the Aussies holding their rifles in one hand and walking sticks for the Kokoda Trail in the other. AWM

A patrol of the 2/31st Australian Infantry Battalion advancing along the banks of the Brown River south of Menari along the Kokoda Trail in October 1942. Both sides continually patrolled in jungle terrain like that seen on either side of the track. Within a month's time, the 2/31st became the first Australian troops to re-enter Kokoda. AWM

Australian troops of the 39th Infantry Brigade march on the Kokoda Trail in August 1942 to meet the Japanese advance over the Owen Stanley Range. Troops arrived in the forward area exhausted after marching for days up and down the mountainous track. The trail was almost always muddy, and the Australian troops either marched with wooden walking sticks or pulled themselves up the slopes by holding on to protruding roots. Their facial expressions so early on did not reveal the deprivations they would suffer in combat and in the harsh terrain of Papua. NARA

Gaunt in appearance, these Australian infantrymen from the 2/27th Infantry Battalion take a respite along the Kokoda Trail at Itiki to have their rations in early October 1942. They had been out of touch with other troops for thirteen days and had very little food when they came in from the jungle. AWM

Three Australian infantrymen from the 2nd Battalion of the Australian 14th Brigade are reunited with their compatriots after being cut off from their main body near Myola during the retreat down the Kokoda Trail in the summer of 1942. NARA

Papuan porters carry supplies up the "Golden Staircase" near the start of the Kokoda Trail leading to Nauro. The supplies were for the Australian infantry fighting the Japanese during the latter's offensive on Port Moresby over the Owen Stanley Range. USAMHI

An Australian Lithgow Bren light machine gun (LMG), the principal LMG for British and Commonwealth forces throughout the war. This particular Bren gun was manufactured at Lithgow Small Arms Factory in New South Wales, Australia. The original Bren Mk I was based on the Czechoslovak weapon, the ZB vz. 26, originally made in the city of Brno, and gave mobile fire support to small groups of infantrymen. Although capable of only a relatively low rate of fire using .303-inch ammunition, it was quite accurate. AUTHOR'S COLLECTION

The Owen Machine Carbine, commonly called the Owen Gun, was developed and manufactured in Australia, reaching front-line troops by early 1943. The majority of the 50,000 Owen Guns were deployed in the Pacific. The gun fired a 9mm (.35-inch) Parabellum bullet, had an overall length of 32 inches, and weighed just over 9 pounds. It had a unique 33-round detachable box magazine loaded from the top and a cyclic rate of fire of 700 rounds per minute. Its range was limited to 230 feet. AUTHOR'S COLLECTION

A British Bren Mk II LMG, which was first produced in 1941. It weighed 22.5 pounds and had an overall length of just over 45 inches. Its cyclic rate of fire was only 500 rounds per minute, but it had a range of nearly 3,300 feet. It was gas-operated and air-cooled and fired the standard British .303-inch cartridge in detachable magazines of 20, 30, or 100 rounds, which loaded from the top of the weapon. AUTHOR'S COLLECTION

The Browning M1919 A4 .30-caliber medium machine gun provided effective infantry fire support and was light enough for rapid displacement under combat conditions. Adapted from the Browning M1917, this machine gun was air-cooled rather than water-cooled and had a cyclic rate of fire of 400–600 rounds per minute with a range of just over 6,500 feet. It was fed with a 250-round belt of ammunition. AUTHOR'S COLLECTION

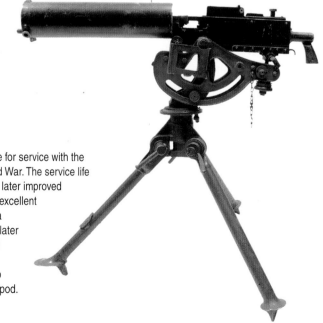

The Browning M1917 A1 was a heavy machine gun produced in time for service with the American Expeditionary Force (AEF) in France during the First World War. The service life of the Browning M1917 extended for more than half a century. It was later improved and designated the M1917 A1, and continued to earn respect as an excellent defensive weapon in the jungles of New Guinea. Initial models fired a .30-caliber round at a cyclic firing rate of 450 rounds per minute, but later designs could reach 600 rounds per minute. It was water-cooled and belt-fed. With a weight of almost 33 pounds, this machine gun was usually situated in a fixed position and required the bulk of its crew to move it for tactical reasons. Here, the venerable M1917 A1 is on a tripod. AUTHOR'S COLLECTION

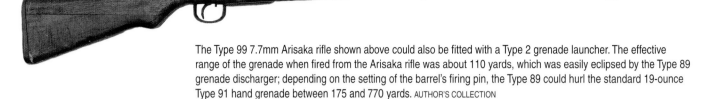

The Type 99 7.7mm Arisaka rifle shown above could also be fitted with a Type 2 grenade launcher. The effective range of the grenade when fired from the Arisaka rifle was about 110 yards, which was easily eclipsed by the Type 89 grenade discharger; depending on the setting of the barrel's firing pin, the Type 89 could hurl the standard 19-ounce Type 91 hand grenade between 175 and 770 yards. AUTHOR'S COLLECTION

The Lee-Enfield No. 1 Mk III SMLE (Short Magazine Lee-Enfield) rifle became the primary infantry weapon of British and Commonwealth forces during WWII. The bolt-action rifle was one of a long-serving series of weapons, with specialized variants active decades after the war. It first entered service in 1907 and fired a .303-inch cartridge. Its ten-round box magazine was loaded with five-round charger clips. This model had a range of over 1,600 feet. AUTHOR'S COLLECTION

A Japanese Type 38 6.5mm Arisaka rifle with its classic Type 30 sword bayonet with hooked quillon and leather scabbard. The training dictum of the Japanese infantryman, regardless of terrain, was to close with the enemy in a bayonet assault. In the purest martial style, they often attacked with fixed bayonets and unloaded rifles in an attempt to intimidate the enemy. To prevent reflection, they frequently covered the blades with mud before combat operations; despite this, many American veterans of the New Guinea campaign reported seeing the flash of bayonet steel during a *banzai* charge. AUTHOR'S COLLECTION

The Japanese 50mm barreled Type 89 Grenade Discharger was a favorite weapon of the Japanese infantry, with three of these fire-support weapons in each platoon. It entered IJA service in 1929 and acquired the misnomer of "knee mortar" because of its curved baseplate. Although it could fire signal and smoke shells, the weapon primarily discharged the infantry's standard 19-ounce Type 91 hand grenade. The Type 89 grenade discharger was operated by a two-man crew. It could send a grenade much farther than a soldier could either by hurling or launching a grenade from his Arisaka rifle. This weapon inflicted an incredibly high percentage of casualties among Allied infantrymen in New Guinea.

AUTHOR'S COLLECTION

A late-model Arisaka Type 38 6.5mm rifle, which was of poorer quality compared to those made before or early on in the war due to Japan's increasing shortage of natural and manufactured resources. Nevertheless, these weapons were still useful to arm the Home Islands' local defenders. AUTHOR'S COLLECTION

The Arisaka Type 99 7.7mm Sniper rifle was issued in 1942 and fitted with either a 2.5X or 4X Tokia telescope. This weapon did not get its own unique number pattern identifier like its forerunner, the Type 97 Sniper rifle, which was a Type 38 6.5mm Arisaka with a 2.5X Tokia telescopic scope mounted on the left side of the receiver behind the magazine breach. In the below photograph, a monopod has been positioned backward to provide a steadier platform for sniping in the prone position. AUTHOR'S COLLECTION

A Browning FN Model 1910 semiautomatic pistol that originated in Belgium during its production run from 1910–83. It weighed under 2 pounds unloaded, fired either an eight-round .380-inch or nine-round .32-inch detachable box magazine, and could be interchanged by attaching a different barrel. This gun was owned by an Australian officer in New Guinea, who procured it while serving on the Western Front during the First World War and used it as a personal sidearm. AUTHOR'S COLLECTION

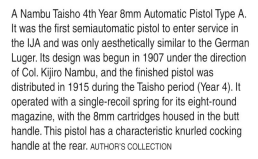

A Nambu Taisho 4th Year 8mm Automatic Pistol Type A. It was the first semiautomatic pistol to enter service in the IJA and was only aesthetically similar to the German Luger. Its design was begun in 1907 under the direction of Col. Kijiro Nambu, and the finished pistol was distributed in 1915 during the Taisho period (Year 4). It operated with a single-recoil spring for its eight-round magazine, with the 8mm cartridges housed in the butt handle. This pistol has a characteristic knurled cocking handle at the rear. AUTHOR'S COLLECTION

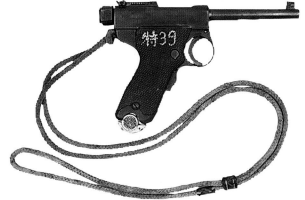

A Nambu Taisho 14th Year 8mm Automatic Pistol, which entered service in 1925. This pistol was a redesign of the Taisho 4th Year Type A, as combat experience necessitated changes in both gun operation and costs. This pistol lacks the grip safety under the trigger guard. It also has a simplified groove pattern on the grips rather than the diamond pattern on the 4th Year pistol, and a three-ribbed cocking handle at the back instead of the usual knurled one. Despite the larger trigger guard, which accommodated pulling the trigger with a gloved finger during the Manchurian winter in the Sino-Japanese War, the gun remained as prone to misfiring as its predecessor. Although an accurate pistol, the rounds were underpowered and had a lowered "knockdown" efficacy.
AUTHOR'S COLLECTION

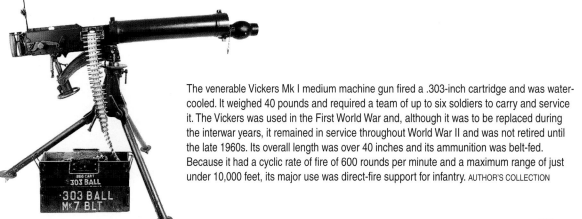

The venerable Vickers Mk I medium machine gun fired a .303-inch cartridge and was water-cooled. It weighed 40 pounds and required a team of up to six soldiers to carry and service it. The Vickers was used in the First World War and, although it was to be replaced during the interwar years, it remained in service throughout World War II and was not retired until the late 1960s. Its overall length was over 40 inches and its ammunition was belt-fed. Because it had a cyclic rate of fire of 600 rounds per minute and a maximum range of just under 10,000 feet, its major use was direct-fire support for infantry. AUTHOR'S COLLECTION

A No. 36 Mills Bomb, or hand grenade. This weapon, produced at the Mills Munitions Factory in Birmingham, was introduced to the British Army in 1915 and was the first fragmentation grenade used by Britain. The No. 36 differed from its predecessors in that it had a detachable base to use with a rifle discharger. It was a grooved, cast-iron, pineapple-shaped grenade, with the grooves enhancing the infantryman's grip, and could be thrown about 30 yards; it had a lethal radius of up to 20 yards. World War II–era No. 36 Mills Bombs had a shorter delay fuse of about four seconds, which proved useful against fortified positions in New Guinea such as pillboxes, rifle pits, and deeply burrowed foxholes. AUTHOR'S COLLECTION

The M5 3-inch antitank gun was developed during World War II in the United States. This weapon possessed the combined elements of both the T9 antiaircraft gun, with its 3-inch barrel, and the M2 105mm howitzer. Released in 1943, its use was compromised by its heavy weight and ammunition-associated problems related to its 76.2mm shell. The M5 had a maximum range of roughly 9 miles and could fire twelve rounds per minute. AHM USAHEC USAWC

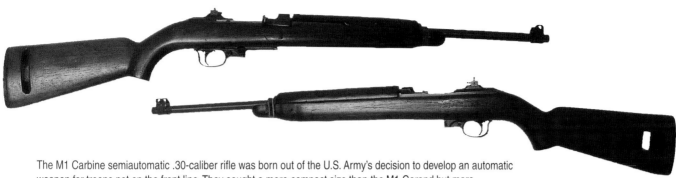

The M1 Carbine semiautomatic .30-caliber rifle was born out of the U.S. Army's decision to develop an automatic weapon for troops not on the front line. They sought a more compact size than the M1 Garand but more effectiveness than a pistol or machine pistol. Its production started in earnest in October 1941; the gun weighed 5.2 pounds unloaded and had a detachable fifteen- or thirty-round magazine. The carbine could fire forty-five rounds per minute, with an operational range just below 275 yards. Although the range and penetration force were less than the M1 Garand's, the M1 Carbine's lower weight and higher firing rate were favorable features for rear area and support troops. By 1945 over 6 million had been manufactured. AHM USAHEC USAWC

The M1 Garand was the standard-issue rifle of the U.S. Army in World War II as well as the first semiautomatic rifle to enter service with any of the combatant nations' armies. It was gas-operated and entered service in 1936, replacing the Springfield Model 1903 bolt-action rifle. The weapon fired a .30-06-inch cartridge fed by an eight-round en-bloc clip through an internal magazine. A skilled rifleman could fire forty to fifty rounds per minute from this stable gun platform with relatively low recoil, giving this weapon the distinction of the highest sustained rate of fire of any standard-issue rifle during the war. It had an effective range of over 1,300 feet; however, it did have a considerable weight of 9.6 pounds (unloaded) as a disadvantage. AHM USAMEC USAWC

The Webley & Scott service revolver, first designed in 1887, achieved widespread use and renown as the Mk VI with the British Army and Commonwealth troops after its introduction during the First World War in 1915. The pistol fired a .455 Webley Mk II cartridge from a six-round cylinder, with an effective firing range of 50 yards, and was rugged enough for the mud and inclement conditions of trench fighting. Many of these guns were still issued to personnel during the Second World War due to a critical shortage of handguns after hostilities commenced. In New Guinea's close quarters, officers favored this pistol because of the stopping power of its cartridge. AUTHOR'S COLLECTION

A Type 94 Japanese officer's sword, based on the long sword carried by the samurai of the twelfth century. The blade could vary in quality from traditional handmade to modern machine-manufactured, but always featured a finely honed cutting edge. The hilt was longer than Western swords and covered with skin from a ray fish or shark, then with leather lacing.
AUTHOR'S COLLECTION

The Arisaka (Meiji) Type 38 rifle was designed by Col. Nariakira Arisaka—although it had a patented Mauser bolt action—in the late 1890s to serve as a substitute for the outdated and expensive Murata rifle. The Arisaka Type 38 6.5mm rifle was first introduced in 1905 and was a five-shot weapon that used an internal box magazine. It was relatively light for its length of over 50 inches, which was considerably longer than the future M1 Garand or M1903 Springfield rifles used by American infantry. Combat experience on the Asian mainland during the 1930s dictated that a higher-caliber infantry rifle was needed, since the heavier 7.92mm German ammunition used by some Chinese soldiers was more effective than the 6.5mm standard Japanese round. Clearly, the 6.5mm Japanese round would not favorably compare to the British .303-inch or American .30-06-caliber cartridges. AUTHOR'S COLLECTION

The Arisaka Type 99—for the year 2009 of the Japanese calendar—7.7mm rifle was initially produced in 1938. The early prototype of the Type 99 had a slightly longer barrel and was heavier than the Type 38. A second prototype, produced in 1939, was shorter (44 inches) and lighter (8.25 pounds) than the Type 38. The longer Type 99 was for infantry and the shorter was for cavalry, engineers, and other specialty troops. However, only a few thousand of the longer Type 99 rifles were produced, and by 1940 it was decided that only the shorter rifle would be issued to all troops. Apart from its size and forward-folding monopod, the Type 99 was identical in construction and operation to the Type 38. AHM USAMEC USAWC

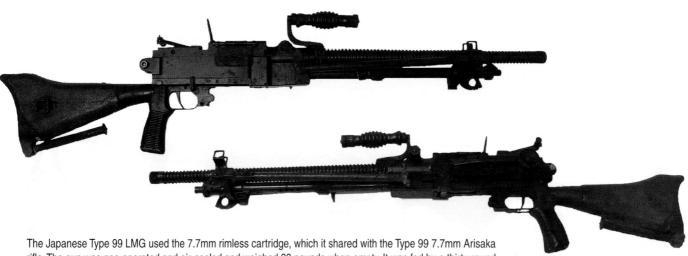

The Japanese Type 99 LMG used the 7.7mm rimless cartridge, which it shared with the Type 99 7.7mm Arisaka rifle. The gun was gas-operated and air-cooled and weighed 23 pounds when empty. It was fed by a thirty-round box magazine that, like the Bren gun, loaded from the top. It had an automatic firing mode only. The Type 99 LMG had fittings for the standard Japanese sword bayonet, and some had the gun behind a detachable metal shield. The gun platform was stabilized by a bipod in the front of the weapon and a monopod under the butt of the stock for sustained fire. It was frequently used in the fixed fortifications in Papua and along the northern coast of New Guinea. AHM USAMEC USAWC

An Australian infantryman looks back on the steep stretch of the Kokoda Trail across the deep valleys toward Ioribaiwa that he has just ascended in September 1942. He holds a walking stick in his left hand and has his SMLE rifle slung over his other shoulder. NARA

Australian troops marching along the Kokoda Trail in an area where there is at least a dirt path with tall kunai grass on both sides. The infantryman to the far left is carrying a Lewis gun of World War I vintage over his right shoulder. NARA

Australian artillery spotters scan for where their shells are landing along the Owen Stanley Range. In addition to mortars, the Australians improvised and developed a short 25-pounder gun/howitzer, which was lighter and more maneuverable in the appalling New Guinea conditions. USAMHI

Three wounded Australian militiamen walk along the Kokoda Trail to a rear area evacuation station. They have already had their wounds dressed, and the medical officers at forward dressing stations have identified the soldiers' injuries on tags pinned to their shirts. If the soldier were unconscious, the tag would identify whether he had received a morphine injection recently so that he was not overdosed. USAMHI

Australian militiamen, members of the Papuan
Constabulary (a native police force), and native Papuan
porters assemble in a village at Eora Creek prior to
beginning their trek up the Kokoda Trail to bring
supplies to front-line troops combating the Japanese
during the late summer of 1942. AWM

Australian infantrymen in their fighting trench attempt
to stem the Japanese advance down the Kokoda Trail in
September 1942. The soldiers are armed (left to right)
with a Thompson submachine gun, a Bren light
machine gun, and a standard SMLE rifle. AWM

An Australian Vickers .303 medium
machine-gun crew provides
sustained suppressive fire while
other soldiers are well-immersed in
their foxholes in fighting at Buna
on January 1, 1943. An infantryman
lies dead next to the Australian
firing the machine gun. The Vickers
Mk I was water-cooled and, at 40
pounds, weighed much more than
the 22.5-pound Bren light machine
gun, making it far less portable in
the jungle. NARA

Allied aerial bombardment caused extensive damage at Kokoda Village during the Australian counteroffensive back up the Kokoda Trail toward Buna in the autumn of 1942. AWM.

Australian soldiers stand at attention as their country's flag is raised at Kokoda Village after the Allied counteroffensive took possession of that locale again in mid-November 1942. AWM

A blind Australian soldier found wounded in the brush after several days is taken down a trail from the Buna sector to an aid station by a Papuan native on Christmas Day 1942. NARA

Australian infantry follows an American M3 Stuart light tank, manned by an Australian armor crew, during an attack through the thick vegetation of a coconut grove to make further gains to capture Buna from the inland approach. LIBRARY OF CONGRESS

Australian infantry are in a line abreast with an M3 Stuart light tank, getting only intermittent cover from the coconut trees of a plantation near Buna. A Bren gunner is firing his weapon from the hip since it was relatively lightweight for a machine gun. LIBRARY OF CONGRESS

An Australian infantry commander jumps on the back of an M3 Stuart light tank to warn the tank commander of a pillbox to the right as the tank gunner blasts away at another Japanese entrenched position. The Australian soldier in the foreground has his sword bayonet attached to his SMLE rifle. LIBRARY OF CONGRESS

An Australian infantryman receives hand grenades from an M3 Stuart light tank crewman through one of the armored vehicle's gun ports. To lighten the loads of the assaulting infantry, the tanks carried extra hand grenades inside the vehicle for infantry distribution; in the coconut groves surrounding Buna, the supply lines were tenuous and had to be improvised. LIBRARY OF CONGRESS

Australian infantry duel at close quarters with the entrenched Japanese using an American M1 Garand with a fixed British sword bayonet and a Thompson .45-caliber submachine gun. NARA

Australian infantry lie prone for the limited cover available as an M3 Stuart light tank fires a high-explosive shell at a Japanese entrenchment at Buna. Most of the pillboxes were impervious to gunfire and mortar rounds and had to be reduced with artillery, tank fire, flamethrowers, or TNT satchel charges thrown in through their firing slits. NARA

An Australian tanker uses a stick to clear mud from one of the wheels on his M3 Stuart light tank during the campaign for Buna in northern Papua. As if the fanatical Japanese defense were not enough, the combat took place in horrific terrain conditions such as the edges of creeks, swamplands, coconut groves, and amid dense undergrowth, often impeding the tanks' progress. AWM

An Australian M3 Stuart light tank commander awaits the signal to continue the attack at Giropa Point in the Buna sector. In this photo, the military censor has blacked out the tank's identification on the hull of the armored vehicle.
LIBRARY OF CONGRESS

Australian stretcher bearers (left foreground) aid a severely wounded infantryman at Giropa Point in the attack on Buna. Advancing Australian infantry and an M3 Stuart light tank are in the background. USAMHI

An Australian soldier hit by mortar shrapnel is given first aid by an Australian medical crew. Using the concealment of tall kunai grass, this constituted a forward dressing station, which was continuously in harm's way. USAMHI

Australian crews in American M3 Stuart light tanks advance in line through the dense vegetation of the coconut grove at Giropa Point, just to the west of the Old and New Strip airfields, in the vicinity of Buna Mission. Again, the military censor has obscured the tank identification markings. LIBRARY OF CONGRESS

Tank crews of the 2nd Battalion, Australian 6th Armored Regiment, step out of their M3 Stuart light tanks during a lull in the action near Buna Mission in late December 1942. NARA

An Australian 2-inch mortar crew
fires a round, using a coconut tree
for protection and to prop up
SMLE rifles with fixed sword
bayonets. This mortar team was
aiming at enemy infantry in
Japanese rifle pits in the coconut
plantation at Giropa Point while the
tank's 37mm gun fired high-
explosive rounds at fixed,
reinforced entrenchments that were
impervious to the mortar rounds.
LIBRARY OF CONGRESS

An Australian 3-inch mortar crew lobs rounds into
Japanese positions 250 yards away at Giropa Point.
Although the round gives off smoke as a marker of its
position, the mortar crew has tried to conceal
themselves in some surrounding fallen branches from
the coconut trees. AWM

An M3 Stuart light tank moves
forward through the rough terrain
of the coconut grove at Giropa
Point. The elevation of the tank's
37mm gun indicates that it is firing
at a target farther away than the
point-blank range typically used to
reduce Japanese reinforced
entrenchments. LIBRARY OF CONGRESS

This tracked vehicle, a disabled Australian Universal Bren Carrier, could carry a Bren light machine gun, a Boys antitank rifle, or a mortar. Later in the war, they were equipped with flamethrowers as well. AWM

An Australian infantryman rests the barrel of his Bren light machine gun on a destroyed coconut tree trunk. He is providing suppressive fire in support of advancing Australian infantry and an M3 Stuart light tank that is charged with eliminating Japanese reinforced entrenchments at Buna's Giropa Point. AWM

Australian armored troops carry one of their wounded on a stretcher while another wounded Australian is hauled on a litter improvised from part of a shelter. The two were injured during fighting at the Old Strip airfield east of Giropa Point and Buna Mission. AWM

Australian troops move through the New Guinea brush with heavy kits and armament since resupply was a constant problem. The lead Australian infantryman carries an Owen submachine gun, also called a machine carbine; developed and manufactured in Australia, it reached front-line troops in early 1943. It weighed about 9.3 pounds and fired a 9mm bullet from a thirty-three-round detachable box magazine that was situated distinctively on the top of the gun and pointed upward. Its rate of fire was 700 rounds per minute with an accurate range of over 230 feet, which was suitable for jungle fighting. NARA

Airlifted Australian and American troops disembark from a C-47 transport for the ground offensive against the Japanese enclave of Gona, which was west of Buna and garrisoned by an IJN detachment. NARA

Two of Australia's finest infantry brigades, the 16th and the 25th, under the overall command of Maj. Gen. George A. Vasey, captured Sanananda and Gona. Here, Australian soldiers take a break in a Papuan village on their trek through the jungle to combat the Japanese naval detachment at Gona in 1942. LIBRARY OF CONGRESS

Australian soldiers clean their rifles in a bivouac area on the edge of a precipice in the Ramu Valley. Operations here were to take control of Lae, Finschhafen, and the Huon Peninsula of New Guinea in September 1943. Troops of the 21st and 25th Brigade Groups of the AIF 7th Division were landed after a flight up from Nadzab to accomplish this task. USAMHI

An Australian 3-inch mortar crew operating less than 250 yards from Japanese positions at Gona. There were at least 4,000 Japanese troops at Gona waiting for the Australian assault in well-fortified entrenchments. Gona had fallen to the Australians on December 10, 1942; however, very hard fighting was yet to come at both Buna Mission and Sanananda Point, the latter situated between Buna and Gona on Papua's northern coast. AWM

An Australian soldier takes his turn to dig a grave for Japanese soldiers killed at Gona in December 1942. Japanese lieutenant general Hatazo Adachi was under Premier Hideki Tojo's strict orders that Gona was to be held to the last man. USAMHI

This group of young Australian brothers who had joined the 2/27th Infantry Battalion hold their SMLE rifles and a Thompson .45-caliber submachine gun (center) and rest on a log after Gona fell in mid-December 1942, over a month before Buna was captured. Gona was important to the Japanese since it guarded their vital landing area at Basabua. NARA

Australian soldiers rest after the final battle to clear the Japanese from Gona in early December 1942. Many had already dropped out of the combat from malaria or heat exhaustion. They also suffered heavy casualties from frontal bayonet assaults on Japanese camouflaged entrenchments and firing pits that put up a withering fire. AWM

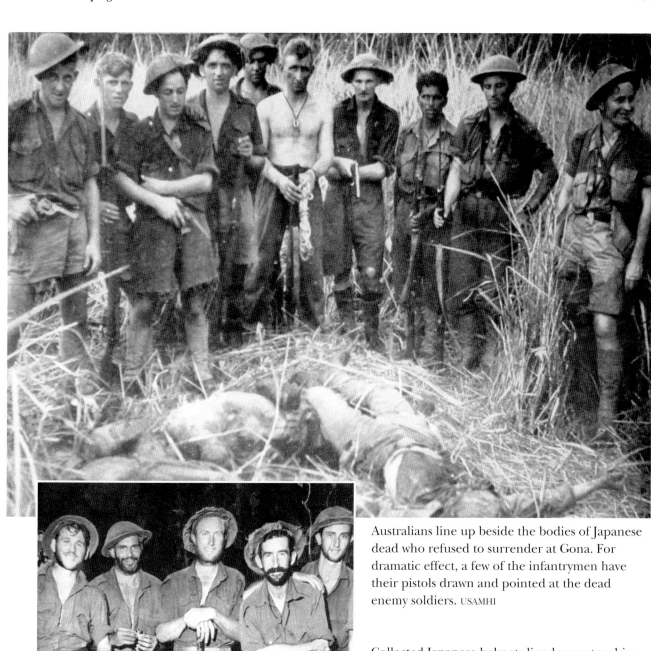

Australians line up beside the bodies of Japanese dead who refused to surrender at Gona. For dramatic effect, a few of the infantrymen have their pistols drawn and pointed at the dead enemy soldiers. USAMHI

Collected Japanese helmets lined up as trophies. The Australian troops showing them off carry the usual assortment of infantry weapons, including SMLE rifles, a Bren light machine gun, and a Thompson .45-caliber submachine gun (far left) used for the assault through the coconut groves at Giropa Point. AWM

Australian soldiers sit and relax, sipping tea from their mugs after intense fighting along the Buna-Gona-Sanananda beachhead's Japanese entrenchments. USAMHI

Air Vice-Marshal George Jones, in the passenger's seat of the lead jeep, and fellow Australian officers, are driven on a tour of the northern Papuan front in U.S. jeeps. LIBRARY OF CONGRESS

Australian troops on the way up through the Finisterre Mountain Range on the way to take Bojadjim on the Huon Peninsula. This was part of the operation to seize Finschhafen on the tip of the peninsula to enable the U.S. Marines and U.S. Army forces to land at Cape Gloucester and Arawe, respectively, on New Britain, where the major Japanese base and the harbor of Rabaul were situated. USAMHI

A captured Japanese dugout near the Buna Airfield camouflages an Australian 25-pounder field artillery piece. Although it was an excellent piece of ordnance, the relatively flat trajectory of this gun often rendered it ineffective at destroying Japanese reinforced bunkers unless the shell penetrated the enemy entrenchment's firing slit. USAMHI

A barge carries an Australian 25-pounder artillery piece, which is mounted on coconut logs, as part of an Australian infantry division's artillery support at Buna in July 1943. NARA

Australian gunners man a 40mm Bofors gun in anticipation of a Japanese air strike after Lae Village, at the eastern base of the Huon Peninsula, was captured in September 1943. NARA

Australians man a short 25-pounder field artillery/howitzer gun. The modification to the venerable 25-pounder made it lighter and more maneuverable for the rugged and wet New Guinea terrain. Ideally, it had a crew of six men and could fire four rounds per minute. NARA

This captured Japanese 70mm Type 92 battalion infantry gun was a complex weapon but provided effective direct- and indirect-fire support. Here, Australian infantrymen use it against Japanese positions at Salamaua, southeast of Lae. Between March and August 1943, the Australian 3rd Division slogged through the jungle-covered hills from Wau to Salamaua. USAMHI

Against no opposition, Australian troops disembark from LSTs at the eastern base of the Huon Peninsula near Salamaua. This landing was to deceive the Japanese that Salamaua was the objective, when the real prize was Lae. The Japanese were tricked and rushed troops out of Lae to reinforce Salamaua. NARA

Australian troops enter Lae on September 18, 1943. All through July and August, the Australians and one RCT from the U.S. 41st Division had placed pressure on the Japanese at Salamaua. On September 4, elements of the Australian 9th Division landed 20 miles northeast of Lae. The next day the U.S. 503rd Parachute Infantry Regiment captured the airfield at Nadzab, 20 miles northwest of Lae, in a *coup de main.* With the airfield seized, the Australian 7th Division was airlifted in, compelling the Japanese to abandon Salamaua and fall back on Lae. USAMHI

Australian infantrymen march past a dead Japanese soldier on the way into Lae. Two helmeted Aussies on the left have their bush hats attached to the webbing on their left sides. AWM

After entering Lae, Australian troops write letters home. Other infantrymen are examined by an Australian medic (far right). NARA

Australian infantry wearily march into Lae on September 18 after the port town was attacked from three sides, forcing the Japanese to evacuate. The Allies wanted Lae since it had an excellent harbor and level, well-drained sites for airfields to assist Admiral Halsey's Central Solomon Island drive AWM.

Australian infantry enter Lae to find heavily damaged buildings and evidence of a hasty Japanese evacuation. MacArthur used multiple axes of assault and deception to deplete Lae's garrison strength before the simultaneous assaults converged. AWM

Matilda infantry tanks (center and foreground), followed closely by Australian infantry, ascend a hill to assault the Japanese-held village of Sattleberg on the Huon Peninsula near Finschhafen. NARA

The Japanese could not linger for long in the inhospitable mountain terrain beyond the Markham and Ramu River Valleys, nor could the Allies leave such a large enemy pocket as Finschhafen in enemy hands. On September 22, 1943, Admiral Barbey's 7th Amphibious Fleet deposited the Australian 20th Brigade on the wrong, but lightly defended, beach to begin the assault on Finschhafen. Here, an Australian soldier carries one of his wounded mates behind a Matilda infantry tank near the village of Sattleberg on the trek to capture Finschhafen. NARA

The 2nd AIF aboard the HMAS *Broome* en route to Buna in 1942. The amphibious operation on the Huon Peninsula in 1943 and subsequent operations were a far cry from the older naval vessels and schooners used to reinforce and supply Buna earlier in the war. NARA

CHAPTER 7
NEW GUINEA CAMPAIGN, 1943–44

MacArthur, in his unending quest to return to the Philippines, wanted to neutralize Rabaul once his Allied forces had taken Lae and Salamaua. To complement the Australian overland advance from Wau through the Markham Valley, roughly 8,000 Australians of the 9th Division made an amphibious landing approximately 18 miles behind the Japanese defenses at Lae, mainly as a feint. In addition, General Kenney's Fifth Air Force's C-47 transports, escorted by 200 fighters and bombers, ferried the U.S. 503rd Parachute Infantry Regiment to Nadzab, about 20 miles west of Lae. The regiment completed the low-level jump in five minutes and secured the landing zone there, meeting no opposition. Within two days, C-47s flew the Australian 7th Division into the airhead. This combined land, sea, and air assault threatened to cut off General Adachi's IJA 51st Division at Lae, so he ordered his troops to evacuate this position and retreat to Finschhafen, 50 miles to the east; it was a disastrous trek that claimed almost 25 percent of the 8,000 Japanese, mainly from starvation.

While Admirals Nimitz and Halsey would advance through the Solomon Islands from the southeast, MacArthur would neutralize Rabaul from the southwest. Rather than directly assault and capture Rabaul, the Combined Chiefs of Staff wanted to bypass this major Japanese base. In order to neutralize Rabaul, Admiral Halsey and his forces had to assault Bougainville—the largest island in the Solomon Islands chain, with its 20,000 Japanese troops—where the enemy was building two fighter airstrips to aid in Rabaul's defense. The task of taking Bougainville fell to the 3rd Marine Division and the U.S. 37th Infantry Division, with the Marines landing there on November 1, 1943. The Marines would be relieved by the Army's Americal (later 23rd) Division under Maj. Gen. Alexander Patch in mid-December. The airfields were captured quickly by the Americans, and Navy Seabees along with U.S. Engineers finished the two strips so that fighter sweeps against Rabaul were operational by January 1944. Despite strong Japanese resistance, Bougainville was secured by March 1944.

To further isolate Rabaul, Finschhafen, the strongpoint that guarded the western side of the 60-mile-wide strait separating New Guinea from New Britain, would need to be captured; this was accomplished mostly by Australian troops and some soldiers of the U.S. 41st Infantry Division. Their assault began at the end of September, but it was not until the end of November that the Huon Peninsula was cleared of Japanese troops. The air bases there would enable Kenney to strike hard at Rabaul, as MacArthur still intended to land on New Britain's western and southern sides at Cape Gloucester and Arawe, respectively.

Simultaneously with the Australian offensive, Gen. Walter Krueger was training his Sixth Army, which ultimately was comprised of the 32nd, 41st, 1st Cavalry, 6th, and 24th Divisions by January 1944. MacArthur also had the 7th Fleet, under Vice Adm. Thomas Kinkaid, and Adm. Daniel Barbey's 7th Amphibious Fleet of transports, cargo vessels, and landing craft at his disposal for future landing operations along the Northeast New Guinea and Dutch New Guinea coasts at Saidor, Aitape, Hollandia, Tanahmerah Bay, and Wakde Island. Eventually amphibious landings would also be mounted against Noemfoor, Biak, Morotai, and the Halmahera Islands, as well as Sansapor on the Vogelkop Peninsula of western Dutch New Guinea. All of these operations would take MacArthur and his Sixth Army closer to his goal of an invasion of the Philippine Islands.

But first, the western end of New Britain had to be seized as part of the neutralization of Rabaul and to protect the Allied flank during the Madang and Wewak operations. On December 15, 1943, MacArthur's forces, the 112th Cavalry Regiment, crossed the straits between Finschhafen and New Britain and withstood dozens of Japanese counterattacks as they landed at Arawe on the western tip of the island on which Rabaul was situated far to the northeast. The 1st Marine Division landed at Cape Gloucester, on the north side of New Britain, on Christmas Day 1943 against light opposition; however, mud, swamps, and dense jungle made an overland strike toward Rabaul impossible. It took the Marines three weeks of marching through inland swamps to secure the Cape Gloucester airstrips. In any event, MacArthur's orders to bypass Rabaul, along with his numerous New Guinea landings, allowed the major Japanese base to be reduced by air attacks and supply interdiction. Furthermore, capture of Los Negros in

A battalion from the 503rd Parachute Infantry Regiment (PIR) jumps at low altitude, amid a smoke screen and a large fighter and bomber protective umbrella, onto a landing field at Nadzab, approximately 20 miles west of Lae, on the morning of September 5, 1943. Meeting no opposition, the paratroopers quickly seized the drop zone to airlift in the Australian 7th Division within forty-eight hours. The combined air, sea, and inland assaults cut off the Japanese 51st Division at Lae from General Adachi's Eighteenth Army forces. NARA

A paratrooper jumps from a C-47 over New Guinea onto the landing zone at Nadzab. The previous trooper's static line is in front of him as he exits the door. This mission was the first one where paratroopers were used in a strategic role; that is, as part of the larger envelopment of Japanese forces at Lae. NARA

As a trooper's parachute opens during the low-altitude jump, another paratrooper exits from the C-47. The entire battalion of the 503rd PIR left their C-47 transports within five minutes. NARA

Once on the ground, the paratrooper rolls up his parachute so that he can more quickly get out of his harness and put together his gear and personal weapon. NARA

After removing his parachute and harness, this paratrooper stands ready with his Thompson .45-caliber submachine gun with a box magazine. The highly accurate jump at Nadzab reportedly convinced General Marshall to allow the U.S. 82nd Airborne's jump in Sicily to go forward; however, friendly fire from navy vessels there wreaked havoc on the transports and paratroopers. NARA

Prior to the jump at Nadzab,
paratroopers of the 503rd PIR get their
weapons and ammunition ready. In the
foreground lay an M1 Garand rifle and
an M1 carbine with a folding open metal
stock. The paratroopers are readying
their ammunition belts for their .30-
caliber Browning machine gun, sitting on
its tripod to the right. NARA

Once on the ground at Nadzab, the crew
of a .30-caliber Browning machine gun
sets up and loads their weapon in
anticipation of the usual Japanese
counterattack; however, they met no
opposition. NARA

Paratrooper gunners ready to fire their 75mm howitzer shortly after the mass descent onto the landing field at Nadzab. Once the airfield was secured, C-47 transports ferried in Australian reinforcements and heavy weapons to defend it. NARA

If a strategic location did not have an existing airfield, MacArthur's planning staff would select a site to build one. Often these airfields were hacked out of adjacent jungle, and crushed coral would be used as a surface. Here, U.S. Navy Seabees add the final touch by laying end-to-end Marston metal matting to complete an airstrip capable of handling General Kenney's medium and heavy bombers. USAMHI

Once Allied airfields became operational, they also became targets for Japanese army and navy fighter and bomber attacks. Here, a .50-caliber antiaircraft machine gun is positioned at an airfield's edge, with appropriate camouflage netting, in February 1943. USAMHI

A 40mm Bofors antiaircraft artillery crew in February 1943 scans the skies for an enemy attack while the ammunition loader readies the next four rounds to be loaded into the gun. In the background, a C-47 is about to land. The crew, always alert for snipers, have their M1 Garand rifles nearby. USAMHI

Since Biak Island was not entirely secured, MacArthur wanted to seize Noemfoor Island, 50 miles west of Biak, with its three airfields. This photograph is an aerial view of Kamiri Airfield on Noemfoor after a battalion of the 503rd PIR jumped on July 3, 1944. Many of the paratroopers, with their white parachutes, are on the airfield's runway below. USAMHI

On July 4, 1944, another battalion of the 503rd PIR was dropped on Kamiri Airfield on Noemfoor. Although it was another low-level jump, many paratroopers landed among American as well as wrecked Japanese vehicles alongside the runway (far right), producing up to a 10 percent casualty rate from the airdrop alone. USAMHI

An American paratrooper is dragged through the mud by his parachute at Kamiri Airfield on July 4, 1944, on Noemfoor Island. As soon as the three airfields became operational, Allied planes situated there could support an assault on the Vogelkop Peninsula at the far western end of New Guinea. USAMHI

The 7th Marines landing on Narrow Beach at Cape Gloucester on December 26. They were already getting a taste of the extremely wet conditions that they would have to campaign through. NARA

A heavily armed half-track moves down the bow ramp of an LST at Cape Gloucester. Its firepower consisted of a 75mm howitzer as well as two .50-caliber machine guns with drum magazines to protect it from infantry or air attack. For this weaponry, it usually had a crew of six. NARA

A Marine machine gunner lies in the underbrush off the Cape Gloucester beaches on the island of New Britain. He has his full field equipment beside him and his .30-caliber Browning Model 1919A4 machine gun as he watches out for the usual immediate Japanese counterattack. NARA

A weary Marine on Cape Gloucester totes his .30-caliber, water-cooled Browning M1917A1 machine-gun barrel over his left shoulder while he carries his M1 carbine as a personal weapon at his right side. The M1 carbine, although not as potent as the M1 Garand rifle, was still well liked for its shorter length, which made it somewhat more suitable for jungle combat, where shorter ranges of fire would be needed. Behind the machine gunner is another of his crewmembers carrying ammunition boxes in each hand. NARA

Marines wade chest deep through a very treacherous swampy area that typified the terrain inland from the Cape Gloucester beaches. The first Marine, emerging from the deeper water, carries a .30-caliber Browning Model 1919A4 machine gun over his left shoulder and an M1 carbine in his right hand as a personal weapon. The other two members of the team follow him, trying to keep the ammunition boxes dry and the tripod from falling into the water. NARA

A Marine patrol led by a helmetless point man who carries his Thompson .45-caliber submachine gun slung over his shoulder but ready for sudden action. Other members of the patrol have their hand grenades close by. Such was the nature of the close combat at Cape Gloucester, where the enemy was often lurking in dense vegetation. NARA

A Marine patrol with their rifles ready and ever alert for Japanese snipers crosses a muddy creek inland from the Cape Gloucester beaches. Largely because of the excessively wet terrain, it took the Marines three weeks to capture the airfields after landing on the western tip of New Britain. NARA

Marines move up along a jungle path on the heels of retreating Japanese soldiers on Cape Gloucester on December 30. Two of the Marines in this column are carrying two .30-caliber ammunition boxes for their Browning machine guns as they work toward capturing the Japanese airfield at Talasea. NARA

A Marine patrol on Cape Gloucester cautiously advances with their heavy field packs and weapons, on guard for Japanese snipers in trees, logs, and "spider holes." The Marine in the foreground is holding his .30-caliber Browning Model 1919A4 machine gun in his left hand, which also has a glove on it to protect him from the heat of the barrel after firing. The barrel heated even though it was air-cooled, as shown by the perforated jacket on the barrel. NARA

A Marine .30-caliber Browning M1917A1 water-cooled machine gun is set up on top of a slit trench. The Marine on the right has his M1 carbine ready to fire as his personal weapon. This crew is preparing to storm a hill that overlooks nearby Borgen Bay in northwestern New Britain. NARA

Marines who pushed through the New Britain jungle from the beaches of Cape Gloucester to capture the airfields there look at a wrecked Japanese plane destroyed in the bombardment that accompanied the landing. NARA

The crew of a Marine camouflaged half-track poses with the vehicle's 75mm howitzer and two .50-caliber Browning M2 heavy machine guns, which were mounted to provide protection against air and infantry attacks. Within thirty minutes after this photograph was taken, four of the crewmembers were injured by a Japanese mortar round. NARA

A Marine 81mm mortar in action in its sandbag-reinforced pit at Cape Gloucester in January 1944; two of the crewmembers prepare to pass the next rounds forward to the tube loader. NARA

Marine 155mm artillery guns of the 3rd Defense Battalion firing at enemy positions on Bougainville, the largest of the Solomon Islands, in early March 1944. On November 1, 1943, the U.S. 3rd Marine Division landed at Empress Augusta Bay on the west coast of Bougainville, bypassing a large concentration of Japanese troops occupying the southern end of the island. After resisting a full-scale Japanese counteroffensive in March 1944, the Americans on Bougainville undertook "mopping up" operations until the Australians took over the area toward the end of the year. NARA

A Marine M4 Sherman tank climbs up the steep far bank of a swampy Cape Gloucester creek. Marine riflemen are in the background ready to protect the tank from Japanese infantry grenades or explosive assault. The patrol's mission was to reduce Japanese fortified entrenchments in the jungle, which, along with the terrain, slowed the Allied advance to the Japanese airfields. NARA

On December 15, 1944, over a week prior to the Marine landings at Cape Gloucester, Admiral Barbey and his Seventh Amphibious Force landed the 1st Cavalry Division's (now dismounted infantry) 112th RCT at Arawe on New Britain's southwest coast. This division was steeped in history and had tremendous élan, making it one of the finest formations in the SWPA. Here, cavalrymen carry their supplies and weapons off a Landing Craft Vehicle, Personnel (LCVP) vessel, passing a stranded U.S. jeep in the process. The LCVP was big enough to carry a jeep as well as infantry. NARA

Cavalrymen of the 112th RCT of the 1st Cavalry Division wade ashore after disembarking from their Landing Craft, Mechanized (LCM), which had a higher back in profile. The LCMs were able to convey bulldozers, medium tanks, or heavy trucks to the landing beaches at Arawe. NARA

Cavalrymen of the 1st Cavalry Division walk through the shallow surf at Arawe on December 15, 1944. They hold their weapons at the ready as they disembark from their LCVP, but met little opposition. NARA

A machine-gun crew of the 112th RCT mans their .50-caliber heavy antiaircraft weapon in a sandbag-fortified and camouflaged pit on the old jetty at Orange Beach at Arawe. These cavalrymen are on alert for a Japanese air attack as a Landing Craft, Tank (LCT) in the background maneuvers to unload its armored vehicles at the shoreline. NARA

Cavalrymen with their rifles ready man a forward post inland from Orange Beach. In the end, the operations at both Arawe and Cape Gloucester did little to neutralize Rabaul other than denying the Japanese the use of the airfields there to intercept Allied Army and Navy bombers; these bombers inflicted severe damage on the major Japanese harbor and garrison there. The captured airstrips were not used by the Allies, nor was a PT base made operational, despite the loss of 2,000 American Marines and soldiers killed or wounded in both attacks. NARA

Three cavalrymen drive inland after landing at Arawe in mid-December 1943. The American soldiers withstood over a dozen of the predictable early post-landing counterattacks and thereby diverted thousands of Japanese troops away from the Marine landing at Cape Gloucester ten days after the Arawe assault. The cavalryman at the left demonstrates one of the classic firing positions for the M1 Garand rifle. NARA

A reinforced RCT (126th) from the 32nd Division lands on the beach in the first wave at Saidor, on the northwest coast of the Huon Peninsula, on January 2, 1944. These American soldiers were trying to trap 12,000 Japanese troops that had been defeated on the peninsula by the Australians, who were still pursuing them. This landing advanced MacArthur's forces about 100 miles farther westward along the northern New Guinea coast. NARA

Elements of the 126th RCT of the 32nd Infantry Division cross a shallow stream near Saidor in February 1944. Once ashore, Brig. Gen. Clarence Martin, commanding the RCT, stayed along the coast rather than trekking inland. The Japanese forces swerved around him through inland jungle trails and escaped capture. USAMHI

LSTs loaded with troops and equipment of the 1st Cavalry Division approach their landing at the Salami Plantation on the island of Los Negros, in the north of the Admiralty Islands chain, on February 29, 1944. NARA

The first wave of the 1st Cavalry Division (G Troop, 2nd Squadron, 5th Cavalry Regiment) in their LVT "Alligators" and LCVPs land on Los Negros on February 29, 1944. The amphibious operation's aims were to secure Seeadler Harbor, an excellent anchorage on the north coast, and Momote airfield on the southern coast. NARA

Soldiers of the U.S. 37th Infantry Division, an Ohio National Guard unit, climb down cargo nets into waiting landing craft for the invasion of Bougainville in November 1943 at Empress Augusta Bay. The U.S. 3rd Marine Division had landed there shortly before. Bougainville was the largest island in the Solomon chain, and the Japanese had already constructed two fighter airstrips to relieve pressure on Rabaul. Capturing these airstrips was the mission of these American forces. NARA

American soldiers try to reduce a Japanese pillbox with a flamethrower, while other soldiers aim their M1 Garand rifles to shoot fleeing Japanese troops on Bougainville in March 1944. The M2-2 flamethrower (far left) was quite effective against Japanese strongpoints and soldiers sequestered in caves; however, its user was always a valued target for Japanese infantrymen. The hazard was only increased because it had a limited range, necessitating a close approach to the enemy. USAMHI

Marines set up their Browning M2 .50-caliber heavy machine gun in the Bougainville jungle and line up their field of fire. The gun was designed in 1933 primarily for aircraft; however, it became a versatile ground heavy-support weapon with its tripod or mounted on a tank. This weapon was air-cooled, as denoted by the perforated jacket at the rear of the barrel. NARA

American soldiers cross a stream on a return trip from a patrol to ferret out Japanese in the Bougainville jungle. In the foreground, one of their fellow soldiers covers their return with his M1 Garand rifle. USAMHI

Marines of the 3rd Division repel a Japanese counterattack in the Bougainville jungle using an assortment of weapons, including a Browning M1917A1 .30-caliber water-cooled machine gun (center), an M1 carbine (background), and a Thompson .45-caliber submachine gun (foreground). NARA

An Australian instructor observes as his two-man Projector, Infantry Anti-Tank (PIAT) team practices with the weapon to prepare for its use against Japanese bunkers in 1944. The PIAT made its debut with the British Army in 1943. The spring-fed launcher ignited the 2.5-pound hollow charge's propellant and sent it hurling toward its target. The shaped charge could travel a maximum distance of just over 1,100 feet, although under combat 300 feet was a more realistic distance. To some, the weapon was bulky and inaccurate; however, it saw use against enemy bunkers when tanks were not available for direct fire. AWM

An American GI patrol is on the alert for enemy snipers as it traverses the bottom of a bitterly contested hill on Bougainville in March 1944. All three soldiers are using the excellent M1 Garand rifle, which, according to some generals, was the best personal weapon of the war. Note the mud is so deep that it is hard to see the soldiers' feet when they are on level ground. USAMHI

An American soldier fires at Japanese infantrymen concealed in ground and log holes. The M1 Garand rifle he is using, in contrast to Allied and Axis bolt-action weapons, was gas-operated and semiautomatic, feeding a .30-06 cartridge from an eight-round en-bloc clip. This enabled the soldier or Marine to produce a rate of fire of up to 50 accurate shots per minute at a range of over 300 yards. This sustained fire overwhelmed Japanese troops using the bolt-action Arisaka Type 38 or Type 99 rifles. The .30-06 bullet provided intense stopping power against massed Japanese counterattacks.
USAMHI

American soldiers crouch low and advance in single file as they move through dense vegetation on Bougainville with their rifles at the ready. In the background, a mortar round had exploded close by.
USAMHI

An American infantry column crosses a creek on Bougainville. The combination of ubiquitous water, swamp, dense vegetation, heat, and insects made the fighting environment horrific. USAMHI

American soldiers use a vine to help them swing across a narrow swampy creek on Bougainville during the winter of 1944. While a fellow soldier stands ready to catch his comrade, others in the patrol remain on the lookout for Japanese. After suffering about 1,000 casualties and inflicting 10,000 on the Japanese, Americans secured Bougainville by the end of March 1944 and handed over to the Australians. USAMHI

The American soldier on the right is getting ready to hurl a hand grenade at a Japanese pillbox. The standard American grenade was a Mark II fragmentation grenade, aptly called a "pineapple," and weighed 1.3 pounds. The thrower would grasp the grenade, pull the split-pin clear with his other hand, and throw it, with a danger area of about 10 yards. The soldier to the left is holding his Browning M1918A2 Automatic Rifle (BAR), which provided semiautomatic fire support to each American squad. It fired a .30-caliber bullet and had a twenty-round straight box magazine. The gun did weigh almost 20 pounds, and this soldier is not using its bipod, which was of dubious value. USAMHI

An Australian soldier looks at a captured Japanese Type 88 75mm antiaircraft artillery gun at Hansa Bay, between Madang and Wewak on New Guinea's northern coast, after the Japanese evacuated the site. When Allied code breakers became aware that MacArthur's landing at Hansa Bay—an excellent natural harbor 150 miles northwest of Saidor—on April 26, 1944, was to be contested by strong Japanese opposition, MacArthur changed his plans and conducted amphibious operation at Hollandia, Aitape, and Tanahmerah Bay. Hollandia was believed to have almost nonexistent land defenses, but an increasing air presence was developing at the airfields there. In February 1944 General Adachi had sent two full divisions, the IJA 41st and 51st,

numbering approximately 50,000 troops, to Hansa Bay, suspecting that MacArthur would attack there since the strongest Japanese garrisons on New Guinea's northern coast were at Madang and Wewak. USAMHI

Three LSTs disgorge American soldiers on a beach near Aitape while other transport and cargo vessels are offshore, protected by warships. NARA

Troop-laden DUKWs speed from an assault transport offshore to the landing zone at Aitape on April 22, 1944. DUKWs had arrived in the SWPA in March 1943 and could transport troops to the shoreline or serve as floating 4.5-inch barrage rocket platforms, giving MacArthur an ersatz naval gunfire presence that was badly needed since the SWPA commander could not get a single warship to provide adequate bombardment for an assaulting force. Four rocket-firing DUKWs comprised a battery, with each one carrying up to 120 launchers. NARA

American soldiers of the most combat-experienced 163rd RCT of the 41st Division, as well as the 127th RCT of the 32nd Division, both refitted in Australia by General Eichelberger, land on Aitape Beach on April 22, 1944. The three closest soldiers are armed with the M1 carbine, a compact weapon for operations in the jungle. However, many riflemen claimed that the gun lacked stopping power, although it fired a .30-caliber bullet. It was a gas-operated semiautomatic like the M1 Garand rifle and weighed about 4 pounds less, even though it had a fifteen- or thirty-round detachable box magazine. NARA

Soldiers from the 163rd RCT splash across a shallow stream near Aitape. After reaching dry ground, they formed into small patrol groups to hunt down lurking Japanese defenders. Aitape was roughly halfway between Hollandia and the strong Japanese garrison at Wewak, so the GIs' mission was to block any Japanese units moving westward toward Hollandia. NARA

The beachhead scene at Aitape with a Landing Craft, Infantry (LCI) in the background and several Landing Craft, Mechanized (LCM) bringing wheeled trailers to the shoreline. The troop-carrying LCI could crawl right up to the beach where the 200 or so men it carried would disembark down a walkway with stairs on either side of the vessel. In almost eighteen months of combat in SWPA, the amphibious assaults now bore no resemblance to the Buna campaign in Papua, where vessels such as wooden coastal schooners were used. NARA

Soldiers of the 163rd RCT on the move in the Aitape area to secure the Tadji Airdrome. However, strong elements of the Japanese Eighteenth Army were making a determined attempt to break through from their Wewak-Hansa Bay garrison to the east with the intent of retaking the Hollandia beachhead and new American base. The Tadji Airdrome was needed to provide air cover and to air transport supplies to Hollandia. NARA

Infantrymen ride on the back of an M4 Sherman tank's hull as they head into the jungle from their landing area at Aitape beach. Infantry and a jeep follow the tank. American ordnance and firepower for amphibious assaults had improved immensely from the 1942–43 Papuan campaign. NARA

GIs reinforce a dugout for their .50-caliber quad mobile antiaircraft battery on a four-wheeled trailer in anticipation of the ever-present Japanese air attack. The Americans landing at both Aitape and Hollandia were fortunate that General Kenney's code breakers knew in March 1944 that about 350 Japanese aircraft were being concentrated near Hollandia, where the enemy believed they were safely beyond the range of Allied air strikes. However, Kenney had a new model of the P-38 Lightning fighter that accompanied sixty heavy B-24 Liberator bombers that demolished nearly all the operational Japanese aircraft at Hollandia on the ground. NARA

GIs of the 163rd RCT ford the shallow mouth of the Driniumor River on foot and in their DUKWs as they move to sever the advance of several thousand Japanese being rushed from Wewak in the east to interfere with MacArthur's amphibious operations at Aitape, Hollandia, and Tanahmerah Bay. NARA

American soldiers of Ted Force, comprised of the 124th RCT of the 31st Infantry Division at Aitape, move on to the Driniumor River to set up a defensive perimeter against the westward-advancing Japanese infantry from Wewak. This formation was ordered to Aitape to fight alongside soldiers of the 32nd Infantry Division stationed on the Driniumor River. General Adachi had planned to breach the Driniumor River line at a point 3,000 yards inland on July 10, 1944, and to envelop the Americans' right flank there with his IJA 20th and 41st Divisions. NARA

A wrecked Japanese "Tony" fighter is examined by U.S. troops on one of the two airfields captured at Aitape on April 22, 1944. NARA

A heavily laden LST with 105mm howitzers and jeeps advances toward the Hollandia beachhead in late April 1944. A .50-caliber Browning air-cooled machine gun is on a tripod on the vessel's deck to defend in the event of a Japanese air attack. NARA

American soldiers attack the Hollandia landing zone in an LCVP while bombs from the covering air umbrella overhead explode near the beach to blast any Japanese positions and send up a wall of water to obscure the defenders' vision of the approaching assault wave. NARA

A crew of the 468th Antiaircraft Regiment sets up their 40mm Bofors gun for airfield protection soon after scizing the field at Hollandia on April 27, 1944. The Bofors gun must have just arrived, since a protective pit with camouflage has not been implemented yet. USMHI

A mortar crew of the 41st Division marches inland from the Hollandia beachhead with their weapon broken down for the trek. Others carry mortar rounds in tubes as well as their M1 carbines as personal weapons against any Japanese hiding in the vegetation along the way. NARA

American soldiers of the 41st Division, which landed at Humboldt Bay, advance toward the Hollandia airfields, which was their primary task. Three weeks earlier, Kenney's Fifth Air Force destroyed over 300 Japanese planes there on the ground. The first two GIs are carrying M1 Garand rifles. LSTs and other landing craft are in the background. NARA

American soldiers await orders after landing at the Hollandia beachhead. An officer is using a "walkie-talkie" to communicate, as an LST has come up to the beach in the background. Most of the soldiers have their M1 Garand rifles slung over their shoulders or, like the officer, have M1 carbines as their personal weapons. The seated soldier in the foreground has a machete on his backpack, which was commonplace to hack through sometimes-impenetrable overgrowth. NARA

American soldiers follow a line of M4 Sherman tanks employing their 75mm turret gun firing either high-explosive or armor-piercing shells to reduce Japanese pillboxes, which were impervious to rifle fire, grenades, and mortar. NARA

A U.S. jeep speeds out from its LCVP at the Hollandia beachhead. An LST is in the background to the right, while several other landing craft are off in the distance. NARA

A line of the amphibious LVT Alligators advances at Hollandia. This photograph was taken through a section of fuselage of a destroyed Japanese airplane at one of the three airfields seized as the mission's goal. NARA

An American soldier, wearing a jungle camouflage uniform, cautiously inspects a native hut on a lake in the Hollandia area for any lurking Japanese soldiers or snipers. Once ashore, the 24th Division, landing at Tanahmerah Bay, and the 41st Division, landing at Humboldt Bay, moved east and west, respectively, in a pincer movement to encircle Hollandia's three airfields. The maze of jungle trails, rain-swollen streams, and swamps were major terrain hurdles to overcome. There were also 7,600 Japanese near Hollandia; however, most were service troops ill-equipped for battle. Others simply fled into the jungle with the hope of trekking to Sarmi, 150 miles northwest on the coast of New Guinea. NARA

LCVPs proceed toward the beach at Tanahmerah Bay, 25 miles northeast of Hollandia, on April 22, 1944, while simultaneous strikes were underway at Aitape and Hollandia. This was a coup for MacArthur, who was assaulting more lightly defended areas—the Japanese did not anticipate his landing there. In this manner, he continued his westward advance along the northern New Guinea coast while "leapfrogging" over strong Japanese garrisons to the east at Madang, Wewak, and Hansa Bay. NARA

Coast Guard–manned LSTs, along with idle LCVPs and LCMs, lined up at Tanahmerah Bay loaded with men and equipment to be disembarked on April 22. NARA

An LCM unloads both American soldiers and a pillbox-smashing tank at the beachhead at Tanahmerah Bay on April 22. The sand at Tanahmerah Bay was very dense, but the 24th Division was expected to advance rapidly. A congestion and supply problem soon ensued since it was impossible to get vehicles off the beach. The 24th Division advanced slowly, with its soldiers having to hand-carry all their supplies; for weeks, they lived on half rations. NARA

An LCM is launched at an assembly yard carved out of the virgin jungle on the northern New Guinea coast. The assembly and maintenance of these vessels fell to the soldiers of the 2nd Engineer Special Brigade, which reached Australia in March 1943. In addition to transporting troops to the beachhead, these craft, along with the larger LSTs, served as floating barracks, warehouses, and hospitals, since during MacArthur's westward advance along the northern New Guinea coast there was an extreme shortage of adequate port facilities. LCMs and LCVPs were used to move supplies and reinforcements for the numerous amphibious operations. These LCMs took part in the Wakde Island landings by the 163rd RCT of the 41st Division on May 18, 1944, 125 miles to the west of Hollandia. NARA

The first wave of elements of the 163rd RCT of the 41st Division hits the beach at Wakde Island on May 18. The previous day, elements of this formation landed unopposed in Maffin Bay near Sarmi. Wakde Island proved to be a much more difficult mission. It took two days of close fighting to wrest the roughly 800 Japanese troops from their "spider holes," coconut-log bunkers, and caves. Stretcher-bearers run down the bow ramp of their LCV in the foreground. USAMHI

The assault wave of the 163rd RCT of the 41st Division comes ashore on Wakde Island on May 18 as soldiers rapidly leave their LCVP. Note the MII "pineapple" hand grenade in the right foreground that fell off the webbing of one of the soldiers. USAMHI

Soldiers of the 163rd RCT of the 41st Division search for cover on the beach of Wakde Island after landing there in mid-May 1944. In the background is the LCVP that unloaded the soldiers at the shoreline. Also in the background is a B-25 Mitchell medium bomber that bombed and strafed Japanese positions in support of the landing. NARA

Americans soldiers at Wakde crouching amid destroyed jungle palm trees to avoid fire from the 800 Japanese defenders. In the background is an M4 Sherman tank out in front of the infantry to silence enemy-reinforced pillboxes that were applying withering fire on the GIs. NARA

Individual American soldiers lying behind standing and fallen palm trees on Wakde Island as the M4 Sherman tank to the right ambles forward to tackle Japanese entrenchments with its 75mm turret gun and .50-caliber machine guns. NARA

On Wakde Island, an M4 Sherman moves forward cautiously while infantry crouch and crawl behind it to prevent enemy infantry from disabling the tank with either hand grenades or explosive charges. NARA

A dead Japanese infantryman, with his helmet and Arisaka rifle beside him, lies near a reinforced rifle pit. IIe was killed by a preparatory naval bombardment before the 163rd RCT of the 41st Infantry Division landed. NARA

A 105mm howitzer crew readies their weapon on Wakde Island to fire at Japanese-reinforced pillboxes made of concrete and coconut logs. Mortars, grenades, and smaller-caliber artillery pieces were wholly ineffective at these entrenchments, as had been aptly demonstrated at Buna in 1942. NARA

Combat medics set up an aid station in the forward fighting area, which was essentially a bomb crater from the pre-invasion bombardment. Over 100 soldiers of the attacking companies of the 163rd RCT of the 41st Infantry Division were wounded at Wakde. NARA

American soldiers of the 163rd RCT of the 41st Infantry Division killed on Wakde Island are identified by medical personnel as they lie under tent half-sheets amid fallen coconuts. Forty American soldiers were killed while 759 Japanese corpses were found; only four Japanese infantrymen were taken prisoner. NARA

An Australian infantry landing party crouches on a sandy beach, waiting to move inland into the jungle on an island off New Guinea's coast in late 1944. With large Japanese troop concentrations remaining on New Britain, Bougainville, and other locales that MacArthur had "leapfrogged" over, the Australian soldiers resented being consigned to "mopping-up" operations rather than playing a major role in a decisive campaign such as the invasion of the Philippine Islands. These infantrymen are carrying their SMLE rifles, or an occasional Owens Machine Carbine or Owen Gun with its characteristic box magazine extending upward from the top of the gun. AWM

A captured Japanese antiaircraft artillery gun is inspected by American soldiers on a beach on Biak Island. Although the first wave of the 41st Division landed exactly as planned, strong currents carried later waves well to the west, which was fortuitous since these areas were less well-defended. In all, the Japanese resistance was minimal as the invasion caught them by surprise. NARA

Soldiers of the 41st Infantry Division follow an M4 Sherman tank on Biak Island. The 12-foot-high scrub growth, along with rugged terrain and Japanese entrenchments in caves, slowed the American advance along the coastal track toward the desired coral airstrips. Upon reaching the airfields, the 162nd Infantry Regiment was driven back by a Japanese counterattack. Fighting raged until the airfields were taken; however, Japanese artillery above the airdrome prevented Allied warplanes from operating there. NARA

Because Biak's airfields could not be used, the 158th RCT (Reinforced) was ordered to assault Noemfoor Island on July 2, 1944, and to capture the three airfields there. Here, a landing wave wades through shallow surf against nominal Japanese resistance. LSTs in the background carried the nearly 13,500 invasion troops. All three airfields were seized by July 6 with light casualties. NARA

American soldiers of the 158th RCT (Reinforced) advance behind LVT Buffaloes as armored support through wrecked Japanese airplanes near Kamiri Airstrip on July 6, 1944. NARA

American soldiers advance through the brush in search of Japanese on Middelburg Island off the Dutch New Guinea coast. The soldiers are astride an amphibious tank, the LVT (A), which was adapted to mount an M3 light tank turret with a 37mm cannon in its turret along with a 7.62mm machine gun to use against enemy infantry and aircraft. This vehicle was intended to provide fire support during the initial stages of an amphibious landing, giving a significant punch in the battle to establish a beachhead. Later, this tracked vehicle would have a 75mm howitzer in its turret since the 37mm gun proved too light for the task. NARA

GIs riding on a LVT Buffalo from a reconnaissance unit on Middelburg Island north of Sansapor on Dutch New Guinea on August 4, 1944. The LVT crew is protecting a flank and keeping a lookout for Japanese snipers. NARA

Soldiers of the U.S. Sixth Army move inland from their landing beach near Sansapor on Dutch New Guinea on July 30, 1944; it was MacArthur's final assault on the world's second largest island. Sansapor was a weak point between two known Japanese strongpoints on the Vogelkop Peninsula. There were about 15,000 Japanese troops of the IJA 35th Division at Manokwari, 120 miles east of Sansapor. Sixty miles to the west of Sansapor were 12,500 Japanese troops at the major airdrome of Sorong. The 7,300 men of the U.S. Sixth Army landed unopposed and seizcd a coastal strip with jungle overgrowth between the two Japanese strongpoints. U.S. combat engineers quickly transformed it into two airfields to provide the necessary air umbrella for MacArthur's invasion of Morotai in the Molucca chain. USAMHI

The invasion force of the 155th Infantry Regiment of the 31st Division wades through the surf to get to the landing beach of Morotai Island in the Molucca chain on September 15, 1944, without any Japanese opposition. In the distance are the LCIs and LSTs that brought in the invasion force. USAMHI

American soldiers cover an entrance to a hut while searching for Japanese soldiers in hiding on Morotai. NARA

African-American soldiers of the 2nd Battalion, 93rd Division (Colored), cross a shallow river, carrying mortar rounds and their M1 Garand rifles, about 500 yards from where Japanese troops are entrenched on the island of Bougainville. African-American soldiers of the 24th Infantry Regiment began to see action on Bougainville in mid-March 1944, corresponding to the start of a large Japanese offensive to eliminate the U.S. Army's perimeter and lodgment at Empress Augusta Bay. USAMHI

African-American soldiers stream down the ramp of an LST near Hollandia on April 22, 1944. They were a part of MacArthur's assault there to secure valuable airfields for General Kenney's airplanes. NARA

African-American soldiers of E Company, 25th RCT, 93rd Division (Colored), field-strip and clean the barrels of their M1 Garand rifles in a bivouac area. The 25th Infantry Regiment, commanded by Col. Everett M. Yon, left Guadalcanal for Bougainville on March 26, 1944, and two days later landed at Empress Augusta Bay, where the U.S. Army's 37th and Americal Divisions had formed a defensive perimeter protecting their fighter strip at Cape Torokina. On March 30, the strip was placed under the control of the Americal Division, which held the eastern half of the perimeter. NARA

Battling heat, insects, vegetation, and the Japanese, U.S. African-American soldiers of the 93rd Infantry Division (Colored) advance along the Numa Numa Trail, which extended from the fighter strip at Cape Torokina to outside the northern side of the American perimeter. NARA

During the combat of April 6, 1944, soldiers struggle to help carry a wounded member of the 93rd Infantry Division (Colored) up Hill 250 under intense Japanese fire. NARA

Laden with their full kits and combat necessities, soldiers of the 93rd Infantry Division (Colored) push through the dense vegetation and swamp of the East West Trail on Bougainville, which connected the fighter strip at Cape Torokina to outside the eastern end of the perimeter. NARA

African-American troops of the 25th Infantry Regiment, 93rd Infantry Division (Colored), advance behind an M4 Sherman tank at Empress Augusta Bay at Bougainville. NARA

An African-American gun crew of Section 1 (Colored), Battery A, 593rd Field Artillery Battalion, prepares to fire their 105mm howitzer on Bougainville on April 16. NARA

An African-American gun crew of Section 2 (Colored), Battery B, 49th Coastal Artillery, loading their 155mm artillery gun on Bougainville on April 18. NARA

CHAPTER 8
AMERICAN AIR AND SEA INTERDICTION

Gen. George C. Kenney was one of the outstanding air commanders of the war. He arrived in Australia in July 1942 and soon won the support and approval of General MacArthur by pledging fealty to the SWPA commanding general. Kenney's assessment was to avoid direct confrontation, especially frontal assaults, against the main Japanese positions, and to seize enemy airfields, especially in lightly defended zones. MacArthur had vented about the previous commanders of the Army Air Corps forces down under. Without an ample naval presence in 1942–43, MacArthur's main striking power was to be Kenney's Fifth Air Force, situated on jungle airstrips rather than fleet aircraft carriers.

Kenney was a Nova Scotian who graduated from the Massachusetts Institute of Technology. He served as the U.S. Army representative at the Curtiss Aircraft plant and then became head of production engineering in the Air Corps Material Division. The SWPA was a horrific theater for the maintenance of aircraft, principally due to the heat and humidity. However, Kenney's expertise in maintenance and scavenging wrecked planes for spare parts enabled his aircraft to remain airborne as the supply chain became more reliable as the war progressed.

MacArthur's army divisions and occasional Marine forces were to seize and hold the areas for the airstrips, to be repaired or built up as major fighter strips and bomber airdromes for Kenney's tactical innovations. These included "parafrag" and "skip-bombing," aerial resupply and reinforcement, use of extra fuel tanks on P-38s to augment their range, and heavy-gunned B-25s for destructive strafing by medium bombers.

An American fighter pilot races from his escort car to his P-38 Lightning. Shortly after his arrival in SWPA, pilots in Lightning squadrons shot down forty-two Japanese fighters in three days of aerial combat, thus beginning the struggle to wrest air supremacy from the Japanese. The enemy had numerous airfields on the north coast of Papua and New Guinea, as well as major remote bases such as at Rabaul and Buin on New Britain and Bougainville, respectively. NARA

A P-38 Lightning comes to rest after landing at Korako Airstrip at Aitape on the north coast of New Guinea in the late spring of 1944. The P-38 was a heavy fighter, carrying two booms that supported the main units of the tricycle landing gear as well as the two engines' turbochargers. The pilot sat in the central nacelle behind heavy nose armament and the nose wheel unit. Its maximum speed was well over 400 miles per hour, and it had a range of 2,600 miles. Its armament included one 20mm fixed forward-firing cannon and four .5-caliber fixed forward-firing machine guns in the nose. It could also carry an external bomb or rocket load of 2 tons. NARA

P-38s start out on a mission against the Japanese. Due to their long range, accentuated by extra fuel tanks, the Lightnings were able to attack installations the Japanese thought to be safe. For example, sixteen P-38 Lightnings stationed on Guadalcanal attacked two IJN Japanese Betty bombers—one carrying Adm. Isoroku Yamamoto, commander in chief of the Japanese Combined Fleet—on the morning of April 18, 1943, over Buin airfield on the northern Solomon island of Bougainville. Both enemy bombers were shot down; Yamamoto's charred remains were later found in the jungle. NARA

Fifth Air Force ground-crew airmen inspect four of the B-25 Mitchell bomber's nose-mounted .50-caliber machine guns. A 75mm cannon can be seen on the lower right portion of the nose, while other machine guns are just off to the side of the fuselage. Additionally, the plane's two standard top turret .50-caliber machine guns could be locked in an automatic forward-firing position. Thus, the ten-gun medium bomber became the prototype for an entire line of bomber-strafers used throughout the SWPA with devastating effectiveness against Japanese ground and sea targets. NARA

One of Kenney's Fifth Air Force B-25 Mitchell medium bombers circles over a Japanese coastal vessel to commence a strafing run with its ten .50-caliber machine guns and 75mm cannon. The ripples of three previously dropped bombs straddle the ship, and the bomb bay doors of the plane have remained open. The power of the B-25 strafers first became clear in early March 1943 when the 3rd Attack Group of the Fifth Air Force delivered a devastating blow to a fourteen-ship Japanese convoy sitting just outside Lae Harbor during the Battle of the Bismarck Sea. A low-level strafing and "skip-bombing" attack by a dozen modified B-25s left every single transport and most of their IJN escorts either sinking or badly damaged. U.S. naval historian Adm. Samuel Eliot Morison referred to the attack as "the most devastating attack of the war by airplanes against ships." NARA

A B-25 medium bomber at sea level demonstrates the anti-shipping assault tactic of "skip-bombing." This technique proved highly effective at interdicting Japanese reinforcement of north coastal New Guinea garrisons. Later models of the B-25 lacked the belly turret—since the strafers and "skip bombers" flew so low that the guns were useless—and had waist and tail guns added to them to continue strafing after the "skip bombs" were dropped as the airplane passed over and pulled away from the target. USAMHI

B-25 medium bombers of the 345th Bomb Group Air Apaches strafe and bomb Wewak on the northern coast of New Guinea on October 16, 1943. The Japanese in their artillery gun pits below near an adjacent coconut grove take cover from the intense firepower that these modified Mitchell bombers could deliver. The U.S. officer credited with upgrading the firepower of the B-25 for these missions was Capt. Paul I. "Pappy" Gunn, who was commander of air transport in Australia. USAMHI

A B-25 medium bomber heads to bomb Japanese positions at Cape Gloucester on New Britain in December 1944 to support the U.S. 1st Marine Division that landed there. These attack bombers often flew at low level in support of the numerous amphibious operations MacArthur was mounting against the northern coast of New Guinea. NARA

U.S. B-25 medium bombers flying low-level bombing runs leave Japanese installations aflame in the Wewak area between Hansa Bay and Hollandia on New Guinea's northern coast. In addition to destroying Japanese planes on the ground, the planes are also bombing the coconut groves, purportedly where the Japanese hid their supply dumps near the adjacent airfields and revetments. NARA

Bombing of Humboldt Bay near Hollandia by Fifth Air Force Douglas A-20 Havocs in late March 1944. Kenney's planes and tactics destroyed upward of 300 Japanese aircraft at this major airdrome complex that was invaded by the Sixth Army in late April 1944. USAMHI

A Douglas A-20 Havoc is hit by Japanese antiaircraft artillery and, out of control, almost collides with another plane in its squadron. The A-20 was the American version of the three-seat light bomber initially bought by France and Britain and known by the British as the Boston light bomber. Later models had a considerably heavier forward-firing armament of up to six .50-caliber machine guns, which fit in well with Kenney's tactic of low-level strafing after the 4,000-pound bomb load was delivered. USAMHI

A Douglas A-20 Havoc hits the mast of a Japanese supply ship after its "skip-bombing" run. The bomb splashes are in the background off to the left. Soon after this photograph was taken, the A-20 crashed into the sea. USAMHI

An American B-24 Liberator heavy bomber over Salamaua, on the northern coast of New Guinea to the south of the Huon Peninsula, on August 13, 1944. Note the smoke coming from the bomb bursts below. This heavy bomber could have a crew of eight to twelve members and had four Pratt & Whitney engines. Its range was limited to about 2,100 miles, but it could deliver a bomb load of over 4 tons. NARA

One of General Kenney's tactics was "parafragging," where his B-25 medium bombers would drop fragmentation bombs that would descend to the targets slowly by parachute and then detonate so that the bombers could be safely out of range when they burst. Here, the Japanese airfield at But on the northern coast of New Guinea is attacked in this manner, as evidenced by the numerous white parachutes. Japanese aircraft are parked and camouflaged in their revetments near the runway. NARA

B-25 medium bombers of the Fifth Air Force parafrag-bomb a Japanese airfield 8 miles west of their stronghold at Wewak on February 3, 1944. Numerous fragmentation bombs descend slowly after being dropped at low altitude against the Japanese fighters lined up on the airfield. Many enemy planes would be destroyed during the war by this method. USAMHI

Allied bombs fall on the runways at Lae, located at the base of the Huon Peninsula. Neutralization of the Japanese air presence at Lae enabled MacArthur to conduct a three-pronged advance: by inland assault, seaborne amphibious landing, and paratrooper *coup de main* at Nadzab. USAMHI

Vunakanau Airfield at Rabaul is attacked by medium bombers dropping parafrag bombs at low altitude for accuracy. Note the Japanese bombers parked in their revetments; they were among many that fell victim to such innovative tactics. NARA

White phosphorus incendiaries ignite over an airfield at Rabaul where two Japanese bombers and a fighter are parked. In addition to its incendiary role, the white phosphorus also blinded the Japanese antiaircraft artillery gunners briefly so that the bombers could make their escape runs more safely. USAMHI

A Japanese twin-engine bomber parked discretely in its revetment at the end of a coconut grove is attacked by the parafragging tactic. The Japanese tried to conceal both their aircraft and supply dumps in the coconut groves. USAMHI

Destroyed Japanese planes litter the airfield complex at Hollandia at the end of April 1944 after Sixth Army troops stormed ashore there to seize the sites for General Kenney's Fifth Air Force squadrons. NARA

U.S. Army soldiers and combat engineers repairing Hollandia's airfields get supplies parachuted to them from the bombers that had been involved in the destruction of the Japanese air presence there. NARA

A U.S. Navy carrier-based Grumman TBF Avenger soars over Tanahmerah Bay as landing craft race for the assault beach on April 22, 1944. The TBF Avenger, after its disastrous debut at the Battle of Midway in June 1942, developed into one of the classic carrier-borne or land-based torpedo bombers of the war. NARA

A pair of U.S. Navy Douglas SBD Dauntless dive bombers, with their bombs evident, move toward their target at Hollandia. Halsey's fleet carriers were instrumental in both neutralizing the shipping and air presence at Rabaul and contributing to the Fifth Air Force's effort to destroy Japanese planes on their New Guinea airfields. NARA

Destroyed Japanese aircraft on the ground near Lae, at the base of the Huon Peninsula in Northeast New Guinea. NARA

The wreck of a Japanese navy Zero fighter lies on a beach on the northern Papuan coastline along with destroyed Japanese landing barges, or *Daihatsu.* USAMHI

An intact Japanese navy Zero fighter abandoned at one of the Buna airstrips in January 1943 after MacArthur's Allied ground forces had reduced the enemy fortifications there. NARA

A motor patrol torpedo (PT) boat off the New Guinea coast looks for Japanese merchant shipping and transports attempting to reinforce the enemy garrisons on the northern coast. With Kenney's Fifth Air Force attacking by day and PT boats going after Japanese coastal vessels at night, a successful interdiction of Japanese reinforcement and resupply contributed greatly to strangling the enemy garrisons on the northern New Guinea coast. NARA

A PT boat machine gunner with his twin .50-caliber weapons scans the skies at dusk for enemy aircraft as the light craft sets out on it nocturnal mission to interfere with Japanese naval resupply off the northern coast of New Guinea. NARA

The crew of PT boat 149 returns to base via a river route near Morobe after their nighttime patrolling in New Guinea during the summer of 1943. NARA

The iconic image of a naval seaman manning his twin .50-caliber Browning machine guns on a PT boat off the New Guinea coast in July 1943. In addition to its complement of torpedoes, the PT boat had only heavy machine guns and occasionally 20mm or 37mm ordnance for an added offensive punch. NARA

CHAPTER 9
EPILOGUE

After the disastrous Philippine campaign of early 1942, General MacArthur needed a victory in Papua for the American leaders to regain confidence in his military prowess. The U.S. Army learned a lot from the Papuan campaign of 1942–43, but at a high cost. Allied losses totaled over 8,500 men killed or wounded. It was clear that in the summer of 1942, U.S. Army units were insufficiently trained in contrast to the Australians, many of whom had served in the Middle East theater.

The New Guinea campaign of 1943–44 comprised two different styles of war. For the Australian infantry it was a war of attrition, as the diggers carried the bulk of the ground combat while the American 32nd and 41st Divisions reconstituted themselves after Papua. During this attrition phase in Eastern New Guinea, through the seizure of Saidor in January 1944, there were over 24,000 Allied battle casualties, almost three-quarters of them Australian. After Saidor, as the U.S. Sixth Army and the U.S. Navy's Seventh Amphibious Force were committed to combat, the battle became one of maneuver. MacArthur's major claim to fame in the strategy of the Pacific War was the technique of "leapfrogging," or bypassing centers of Japanese resistance and going on to capture weaker areas at a lower cost in lives. After Hollandia, Allied losses were reduced to 9,500 battle casualties, mostly American. The war of maneuver, along with the "leapfrogging" technique, enabled the Allies to advance more than 1,300 miles in just over three months' time, allowing MacArthur to regain his aura as a masterful tactician and theater commander. His eyes now turned to the Philippines to deliver on his promised return.

Australian forces engaged in controversial operations against the Japanese during the final months of World War II. Although early on in 1944 MacArthur said that he intended to use the three AIF infantry divisions (the 5th, 7th, and 9th) that had served in both the Middle East and New Guinea campaigns in his assault on the Philippines, these veteran units were not included in his invasion plans. It seemed to General Blamey, CIC of the Australian Army, that MacArthur wanted only American units to take part in his triumphant return. With MacArthur's invasion of Leyte, large Japanese troop formations—almost 200,000 troops in total—remained on New Britain, Bougainville, in the Aitape-Wewak area of Northwest New Guinea, and on Borneo. The war ended with the use of Australian soldiers in these controversial campaigns; the troops believed that they were involved in only "mopping-up" operations that were of no importance to ending the war with Japan.

General MacArthur, his staff, and Philippine president Manuel L. Quezon walk through the surf onto the landing beach at Leyte on October 20, 1944.
NARA

General MacArthur signed the surrender document aboard the USS *Missouri* in Tokyo Bay on September 2, 1945. Behind MacArthur stand American general Jonathan Wainwright, who surrendered the American and Filipino forces to the Japanese in the spring of 1942, and British general Arthur Percival, who surrendered Singapore on February 15, 1942, to Japanese general Tomoyuki Yamashita.
NARA

An abandoned Japanese ordnance dump at Hollandia showing machine guns, ammunition boxes, and other supplies. After being bypassed at several points by MacArthur, Japanese Eighteenth Army Gen. Hatazo Adachi, stationed at Wewak, ordered many of his troops into the jungles and mountains of New Guinea to continue fighting. Most died from starvation, disease, and suicide. USAMHI

Japanese prisoners of war captured at Tanahmerah Bay during MacArthur's bold maneuver to seize Hollandia's airfield complex are brought to Finschhafen, previously captured by the Australians, on June 2, 1944. USAMHI

Indian soldiers captured by the Japanese at Singapore and on Malaya are released by American troops from captivity at Hollandia on April 25, 1944. Many of these Indian prisoners of war were impressed into construction projects for the Japanese. USAMHI

Papuan natives upon their release from Japanese labor captivity on Noemfoor Island off the coast of Dutch New Guinea in early July 1944. USAMHI

Gen. George Vasey of the AIF decorates hundreds of Papuan natives who served with the Australians as part of the Papuan Constabulary or as native bearers during the arduous Kokoda Trail and Buna campaigns. LIBRARY OF CONGRESS

In November 1944, Australian
soldiers view some Japanese soldiers
killed on Bougainville. The
Australians took over the perimeter
at Empress Augusta Bay from the
Americans, who had entered into an
"unofficial truce" with the Japanese
on the island. Many Australian
soldiers believed they were doing
solely "mopping-up" operations
rather than making more
substantive military contributions.
Note the Australian soldier on the
left holding his country's Owen
submachine gun. NARA

A Matilda Infantry tank crewed by
armored troops of the Australian
7th Division, veterans of the Middle
East, traverses difficult terrain on
the island of Borneo. A destroyed
oil refinery stands in the
background. The rich natural
resources of the East Indies were a
primary objective of the Japanese
early in World War II. General
Blamey viewed the Borneo invasion
as unnecessary. The only reason for
capturing this island was to use it as
a base for the invasion of Java, but
as American forces were already
near Japan's Home Islands, an
assault on Java had little practical
importance at this late stage of the
Pacific War. NARA

An Australian graveyard at Gona, which the diggers, along with some elements of the U.S. 41st Division, captured in mid-December 1942, a month before the fall of Buna in northern Papua. USAMHI

Maj. Gen. F. H. Berryman of the AIF, commanding the Australian II Corps, turns into the Allied cemetery to commemorate the fallen at Finschhafen on the tip of the Huon Peninsula on February 20, 1944. The Japanese put up fierce resistance at Finschhafen, but the Australians finally subdued them, capturing the peninsula in the process. USAMHI

BIBLIOGRAPHY

Eichelberger, R. L. *Our Jungle Road to Tokyo.* Nashville: Battery Classics, 1989.

Gailey, H. *MacArthur Strikes Back: Decision at Buna: New Guinea 1942–1943.* Novato, CA: Presidio Press, 2000.

Gailey, H. A. *MacArthur's Victory: The War in New Guinea, 1943–1944.* New York: Presidio Press, 2004.

Mayo, L. *Bloody Buna.* Garden City: Doubleday & Co., Inc., 1974.

Milner, S. *Victory in Papua.* Harrisburg: National Historical Society, 1993.

Perrett, G. *There's A War to be Won: The United States Army in World War II.* New York: Ballantine Books, 1991.

Taffe, S. R. *MacArthur's Jungle War: The 1944 New Guinea Campaign.* Lawrence: University of Kansas Press, 1998.

Vader, J. *New Guinea: The Tide is Stemmed.* New York: Ballantine Books, 1971.

ACKNOWLEDGMENTS

I would like to thank the archivists at the United States Army Military History Institute (USAMHI) in Carlisle, Pennsylvania, along with those at the Still Photo Section at the National Archives Research Administration (NARA) in College Park, Maryland, for their help in locating the many photographic files used in the preparation of this book.

I am very grateful for the editorial guidance of David Reisch and the editorial assistance of Brittany Stoner at Stackpole Books, as well as to Philip Schwartzberg of Meridian Mapping in Minneapolis, Minnesota, for his cartographic expertise. Also, I will always have fond collegial memories of the late M. David Detweiler who, with his great enthusiasm for military history, made this book happen.

Finally, as one of the numerous physicians who takes care of many Second World War veterans, who are becoming a dwindling cadre due to the inexorable march of time, we listen to your heroic accounts and read about your gallant exploits, lest we forget.